WISDOM

FROM THE *earth*

ANNA VOIGT & NEVILL DRURY

WISDOM
FROM THE *earth*

The Living Legacy

of the Aboriginal

Dreamtime

SHAMBHALA

Boston

1998

To my son and my Aboriginal nephews and to future generations of children. May they know that under the skin we are all one — and may they live in harmony like the colours of a rainbow.

Anna Voigt

WISDOM FROM THE EARTH

Shambhala Publications, Inc.
Horticultural Hall, 300 Massachusetts Avenue, Boston, MA 02115
http://www.shambhala.com

Text © Anna Voigt and Nevill Drury 1997

First published in Australasia in 1997 by Simon & Schuster Australia
20 Barcoo Street, East Roseville NSW 2069

A Viacom Company
Sydney New York London Toronto Tokyo Singapore

9 8 7 6 5 4 3 2 1

First Shambhala Edition

Printed in Singapore

This edition is printed on acid-free paper that meets the
American National Standards Institute Z39.48 Standard.

Distributed in the United States by Random House, Inc., and
in Canada by Random House of Canada Ltd

Library of Congress Cataloging-in-Publication Data

Voigt, Anna.
   Wisdom from the earth: the living legacy of the Aboriginal
   dreamtime / by Anna Voigt & Nevill Dryry. — 1st Shambhala ed.
      p. cm.
   Includes bibliographical references and index.
   ISBN 1-57062-325-2 (PBL.: alk. paper)
   1. Australian aborigines—Social life and customs. 2. Mythology,
   Australian aboriginal. 3. Australian aborigines—Religion.
   I. Drury, Nevill, 1947–   . II. Title.
   GN666.V67 1998   97-52340
   305.89'915–DC21   CIP

Endpaper: photography by Anna Voigt
Picture research: Anna Voigt
Designer: Handpress Graphics and Anna Voigt
Printer: SNP Printing

CONTENTS

ACKNOWLEDGMENTS

First and foremost our heartfelt gratitude towards Aboriginal peoples who, through their commitment to their oral cultures and love of the land, maintained the health and beauty of this continent for hundreds of millennia. Also for their generosity and willingness to share their knowledge without which a book such as this would not be possible.

Numerous people have assisted us in the course of this project for which we are very grateful as the book would not have reached completion without this support.

Special thanks to Linda Burney and Nigel Parbury of the Aboriginal Education Consultative Group for reading and advising on the manuscript despite their very demanding schedules.

Thankyou to David Mowaljarlai and Jutta Malnic for permission to use the Bandaiyan drawing and extracts from *Yorro Yorro* (1993) published by Magabala Books, Broome, Western Australia, and to Guboo Ted Thomas for the contribution of his extract 'Renewing of the Dreaming'. We would also like to acknowledge the use of short extracts from the works of the following people: James Barripang, Patrick Dodson, Muta, Nganyinytja, Eddie Kneebone, Mudrooroo, Oodgeroo Noonuccal, Thompson Nganjmirra, Wesley Nganjmirra, Sam Woolagoodja, Bill Neidjie, Anne Pattel-Grey, Yami Lester, Galarrwuy Yunupingu, Stephen Page, Bill Harney, Kathleen Petyarre, Felix Holmes and others who are acknowledged in the text.

Special thanks also to senior Law women and artists, Matingali Bridget Matjital and Mirlkitjungu Millie Skeen, for the contribution of their works and stories. We would also like to thank the other Aboriginal artists whose works are reproduced here: Paddy Fordham Wainbarrnga, Djawida, David Mowaljarlai, Freddie Timms, Elizabeth Djarrkman, Beerabee Mungnari, Lily Karedada (Mindindil), Beerabee Mungnari, Warnngayirriny (Jack Britten), Rover Thomas (Joolama), Johnny Mosquito Tjapangarti, Emily Kame Kngwarreye, Philip Gudthaykudthay, Maggie Napangardi, Bobby Nganjmira, Dave Pwerle Ross, Patric Mudjana, Robin Nganjmira, Gloria Temarre Petyarre, George Milpurrurru and Jeremiah Galngarr.

We are grateful to the following art galleries, organisations and photographers for supplying slides and transparencies for reproduction in this book: Adrian Newstead, Katherine Sherer and Margo Bavinton from Coo-ee Aboriginal Art, Sydney; Peter Harrison from Kimberley Aboriginal Art, Melbourne; Christopher Hodges from Utopia Art, Sydney; Bryan Hooper from

Coventry Gallery, Sydney; Manungka Manungka Women's Association, Wirrimanu (Balgo Hills), Western Australia; the Yuelamu community, Mount Allen, Northern Territory; Sandy Edwards of Stills Gallery, Sydney, for photographic advice; Philip Quirk and Grenville Turner from Wildlight Photo Agency, Sydney. Special thanks to our friend, Djon Mundine, for sharing his knowledge.

Individual artworks are credited in the picture captions and photographers works are credited in the Photographic Credits at the back of this book.

There are images and references in this book to Aboriginal people who have died, either before or during the course of this project, and though this may cause distress to members of their communities, they have been included because of their importance in Australia's cultural history. In addition, we advise readers to approach this material with sensitivity and respect for Aboriginal culture in any encounters with Aboriginal people.

We would like to thank the following publishers for the use of copyright material:
Allen & Unwin, Sydney, for extracts from Diane Bell, *Daughters of the Dreaming* (1989).
The Australian Government Publishing Service for extracts from Oodgeroo Noonuccal and Kabul Noonuccal, *The Rainbow Serpent* (1988).
HarperCollins Publishers, Sydney, for extracts from Oodgeroo Noonuccal, *Stradbroke Dreamtime* (1993).
HarperCollins Publishers, London, for extracts from Mudrooroo, *Aboriginal Mythology* (1993).
Spinifex Publishers, Melbourne, for an extract from Catherine Ellis and Judith Martyn Ellis' 'The Sung World of Aboriginal and Islander Women' in *Australia for Women* (1994), edited by Susan Hawthorne and Renate Klein.

Every effort has been made to locate the sources of quoted material and to obtain authority for its use. If some sources have been inadvertently overlooked and later come to notice, they will be included in future editions of this book.

Finally we would like to express our appreciation and thanks to Jon Attenborough for his belief in the book and to our editor, Narelle Walford, and co-designer, Craig Peterson (of Handpress Graphics), for their valued contributions well beyond the call.

Law...

Aborigine can't make law

It come from long time ago.

From the first time.

It can never change.

Always the same.

Our culture can never change,

Our law can never change.

Only people can change.

They born...

They die.

But law stays the same.

Each person is responsible for law,

For culture.[1]

INTRODUCTION

Aboriginal culture now enjoys a higher international profile than it ever has before. While the spiritual roots of Aboriginal traditions lie in the timeless past of the Dreamtime, these traditions are still a living reality in the lives of Aboriginal and Torres Strait Islander peoples today. Many of these people are now sharing their values and perceptions with the world, in this way infusing the contemporary consciousness with a new sensibility.

Clearly there is now a widespread international awareness of Aboriginal music, art and dance traditions, and Aboriginal people also celebrate their achievements in the fields of sport, literature, law and politics — these expressions are integrated with their ongoing struggle for land and the right to self-determination. One has the sense that, from every direction, an Aboriginal voice now demands to be heard as the indigenous cultures of this ancient land seek to throw off the shackles of the white invader's dominating identity. But this is not an act of political insurrection so much as a statement of purpose and identity. Aboriginal peoples across the country seek increasingly to stand alongside other cultural groups in Australia in a spirit of mutual consideration, reconciliation and equality and with due respect for their cultures.

This struggle has been hard fought and is certainly not yet won. It was not until the referendum of 27 May 1967 that Aboriginal residents were granted full legal status as Australian citizens — an extraordinary irony when one considers that Aboriginal peoples occupied this land for tens of thousands of years prior to white settlement. And regrettably there are still substantial pockets of racism in white Australian society. Thirty years after the referendum many Aboriginal people are still subjected to ongoing discrimination and prejudice in many areas across Australia. There also appears to be a persistent view amongst some white Australians that the apparent gulf between ancient Aboriginal traditions and the urban-oriented western lifestyle is perhaps too difficult to bridge. However, this is not a view held by many Aboriginal people themselves, for they are rightly proud of their spiritual and cultural traditions and wish to preserve them for future generations of Australians — both black and white. As a consequence, a number of Aboriginal spokespeople working in different fields have taken it upon themselves to attempt to bridge the gulf between the two cultures. Australia can only become richer for this experience.

What all of these eminent Aboriginal people have in common — politicians, musicians, story-tellers, lawyers, educators, poets, visual and performing artists, writers and sports people alike — is a shared sense of their Aboriginal heritage and a profound sense of belonging to a culture which, in terms of its historical continuity, is the oldest on the planet. Yet characteristic of Aboriginal cultures is an ability to respond to the changed social and political climate of contemporary times while remaining true to the fundamental roots of their cultures. While many of these individuals participate in contemporary forms of cultural communication, the substance and spirit of their expressions, in various ways, continues to honour their heritage. Although on the surface things appear to have changed for most Aboriginal people in the last 200 years, it is also apparent that their fundamental world view remains essentially unchanged. Contemporary Aboriginal Australians are proud of their lineage and often see their chosen fields of endeavour as ways of preserving and creating a wider awareness of their ancient cultural traditions in the modern world.

Prior to the intense current focus on native title land rights issues, perhaps one of the main areas of re-awakening consciousness of Aboriginality in present-day Australia has been the increased recognition of contemporary Aboriginal art. It is important to recognise, though, that the roots of Aboriginal visual expression are as old as the culture itself, and extend back for thousands upon thousands of years — as revealed in their ceremonial lives and in the legacy of their rock paintings. Indeed, it is rock painting and the techniques employed by scientists in dating it which have been utilised in attempts to establish the duration of Aboriginal life on this continent. While the bark paintings of Arnhem Land and the dotted fields of acrylic on canvas produced by Central Desert artists may be the most widely known contemporary Aboriginal art forms, rock painting is their oldest surviving art and is widely found throughout the country. Precisely how old the most ancient sites actually are is currently very controversial because of disagreements which have arisen in response to the most recent discovery of rock art engraving sites at Jinmium in the Northern Territory. However, the macropod track at Olary in South Australia, which was discovered prior to Jinmium, has been dated as 34,000 years old, confirming it as the oldest dated rock art engraving site in the world. It is thought likely that there has been continuous Aboriginal settlement on this continent for at least 50,000 years, and perhaps more than 100,000 years. Aboriginal people themselves believe that they have lived on this continent since the beginning of time — that is, the active part of Creation known as the eternal Dreamtime.

Added to this debate is the controversy surrounding the elegant and mysterious 'Bradshaw figures' found in a number of rock art galleries in the Kimberley region of Western Australia, which precede the famous Wandjina figures also located in this region. The Bradshaw figures appear to be even more ancient than the famous Lascaux cave paintings in France.[2] These painted forms are named after the first European to see them — Joseph Bradshaw — in 1891, and are extraordinary for their unique, very accomplished style. The Bradshaw figures appear to utilise a technique of colour bonding and fine brush painting which differs from current Aboriginal practices. Indeed, there are disputes between Aboriginal people themselves as to their origins, and also with regard to the origins of the people who created them, especially since one of the rock paintings depicts figures rowing in a high-prow canoe.

Whether or not north-western Australia had an ethnically diverse population some 20,000 years ago, or whether the Bradshaw paintings belong to an earlier epoch in Aboriginal visual expression, there is no doubt that the nation's rock painting galleries are an important part of Australia's cultural heritage. It is an Aboriginal ritual custom and responsibility to maintain these sites in good condition, and for this reason rock painting and Australia's cultural history are interconnected. Fine examples of Aboriginal painting may be found in numerous cave galleries and on rock outcrops at various far-ranging sites: from the magnificent Wandjina figures in the Kimberleys to the linear ground figures of ancestral beings, animals, birds and spirits found in the Sydney and Hawkesbury River areas and the extensive sites in the Laura district of Cape York Peninsula. Some cave sites are considered 'secret–sacred' according to Aboriginal religious beliefs, and taboos may still be maintained in certain cases, prohibiting these images from being viewed by uninitiated men and women, not to mention the general public. It is profoundly regrettable that many mining and property developments have had a devastating effect on rock galleries and other sacred sites. More recently, conservation programmes have been implemented, and sites suitable for tourist appreciation have been made available.

When one refers to 'Australian Aboriginal peoples' it is important to remember that this term includes not only the mainland population but also the Aboriginal residents of the islands within the Torres Strait — the stretch of water which lies between Australia and Papua New Guinea. There is also considerable diversity in cultural expression among these indigenous groups, at the same time as sharing a common core of values — particularly in relationship to the Earth and to their Spirit Ancestors. The people who nominated their heritage as 'Aboriginal and Torres Strait Islander' in the 1994 National Aboriginal and Torres Strait Islander Survey numbered 303,300. (In 1996 the total Australian population was estimated at close to 18.5 million.) More recent statistics are not yet available. However, these figures reveal the dramatic drop in the Aboriginal population which has occurred since the time of white settlement: it is estimated that prior to the 1788 European invasion, the Aboriginal and Torres Strait Islander population ranged between 750,000 and possibly up to 3 million. The exact figure is difficult to estimate accurately because of the considerable number of unreported deaths — 'disappearances', massacres and cases of terminal illness. In any case, the decimation of the Aboriginal population from all causes was, and continues to be, a tragedy which can no longer be overlooked in the nation's history.

Ethnographic evidence shows that there were once around 600–700 Aboriginal clans sharing a common language or dialect. Families sharing descent from a common Ancestor formed clans in the first instance, and a clan could have up to approximately 50 members. There are no 'clans' (land-owning groups) as such in certain areas — such as the Western Desert where groups are termed 'bands'; that is, land 'users' rather than 'owners'. A comparable term to 'clan' — and perhaps a more accurate one — is 'estate group', which includes all people with any rights to a given area, whether paternally or maternally inherited. The estate is the area owned by a clan or estate-group, and there are three kinds of rights regarding their ownership of this land: the right to have access to the resources of an area — both material and spiritual; the right to authorise other people to use those resources; and the third is the right to be consulted about an area and anything that occurs there. Exercising these rights varies with a person's age, sex and, most importantly of all, the level of religious knowledge that an individual possesses with regard to the ceremonies, songs and myths associated with different sites in the area.

Traditional Aboriginal people were multilingual and it would seem that there were originally around 300, and possibly up to 500, Aboriginal languages and some 600–700 dialects, all of which appear to be generically related. It is of great concern that today many Aboriginal languages face the threat of extinction. At a rough estimate, only 10 per cent of Aboriginal people still speak their indigenous languages, and of the original 270 or so distinct languages, two-thirds (about 160) are either extinct or have only a handful of elderly speakers remaining. Only around twenty of the surviving languages are actively transmitted to children and adults. The other 70 remaining languages are weakening and are no longer transmitted to or spoken fluently by the younger generations. In areas like coastal New South Wales, Tasmania and Victoria, most of the Aboriginal people were eventually deprived of any opportunity to retain their language, despite the fact that language by its very nature is intrinsic to identity and communication within one's web of relationships. However, present generations are showing an interest in trying to recover their indigenous languages from nineteenth century historical records, and in some instances from the remaining speakers, and are endeavouring to teach these 'lost' languages to classes of adults and children.

In some instances the threatened languages are being replaced by Aboriginal English, a more dominant Aboriginal language, or a creole language known as 'Kriol'. These languages, including Torres Strait Creole, are playing increasingly important roles as lingua francas within and between communities. These languages, although sometimes regarded as simplistic, quaint or 'bad' English, are in fact sophisticated languages adapted to the expression of many traditional concepts and are an important means of marking Aboriginal identity. Most contemporary Aboriginal languages have alarmingly small numbers of speakers — the largest languages are estimated at 3,000–4,000 speakers and include the Western Desert language varieties, Arrernte and Warlpiri, while roughly half of the surviving languages have only 10–100 fluent speakers.

Aboriginal peoples have been largely dispossessed by the process of European invasion, colonisation and economic 'development'. This dispossession occurred first on the south-eastern coast and was replicated repeatedly as the moving frontier of the colonising process gradually encompassed the whole country. State governments retained separate control of their Aboriginal populations until 1967, when a referendum was passed which gave the Commonwealth power to make laws for Aboriginal people in the states as well as in the federally controlled territories of the Northern Territory and the Australian Capital Territory. Aboriginal peoples were not granted the right to vote until 1962, and were not included in the national census until the 1967 referendum, which, as previously mentioned, conferred citizenship and recognised Aboriginal peoples officially as 'Australian'.

Historical sources indicate that following colonisation successive governments intended to wipe out Aboriginal societies, regarding them as 'uncivilised' and consequently of little value. This was attempted in a number of ways. The brutal practices committed against Aboriginal people by colonial governments and a number of white pastoralists and squatters — including widespread massacres in some regions — mark the often inhumane history of white occupation of this land. In addition, diseases were brought in by the settlers against which indigenous peoples had no immunity, and this also resulted in many of them dying.

As if seeking to rectify ongoing institutional practices of discrimination and abuse, various government policies — both state and national — were established between the 1880s and 1930s and referred to benignly by such terms as 'protection' and later 'assimilation'. These policies determined the physical fate of Aboriginal peoples across the land. One needs to distinguish between 'assimilation' and 'integration' because they are sometimes confused and they are not the same thing. Assimilation, unlike integration, is a process by which a dominant cultural group absorbs a suppressed group into its society with the ultimate effect of destroying the subjugated society. Integration, on the other hand, occurs when societies evolve and diversify and benefit from the merging and interaction. From the 1930s through to the late 1960s official bodies pursued a policy of assimilation under the guise of 'protection' and decreed who was suitable or unsuitable for assimilation: 'full bloods' and those not engaged in servile duties were segregated into reserves and the remainder absorbed into the community.

Many people were displaced under this policy, one of the more insidious practices being the forced removal of children from their parents and families and relocating them in white institutions such as orphanages, missions and foster homes. The child captives were then indoctrinated in the values of the dominant culture. This devastating policy of child removal, affecting most Aboriginal families across the continent, continued until 1969 in New South Wales and even later in some other states. A handful of these children — known today as 'the stolen generations' — have tracked down their parents, though thousands have never returned to their homes. This has resulted in a trail of tears of irretrievable and incalculable loss: whole generations have been torn from their families and have become alienated from their own cultures.

At the time of writing, the Australian Human Rights and Equal Opportunity Commission has just published the findings and recommendations of their extensive 'National Enquiry into the Separation of Aboriginal and Torres Strait Islander Children from their Families' in a volume called *Bringing Them Home*.[3] The report opens with a statement that: 'Grief and loss are the predominant themes of this report. Tenacity and survival are also acknowledged.' And further: 'For individuals, their removal as children and the abuse they experienced at the hands of the authorities or their delegates have permanently scarred their lives. The harm continues in later generations, affecting their children and grandchildren.' Following these opening comments is a statement by the Governor General, Sir William Deane, in 1996, which begins:

> It should, I think, be apparent to all well-meaning people that true reconciliation between the Australian nation and its indigenous peoples is not achievable in the absence of acknowledgement by the nation of the wrongfulness of the past dispossession, oppression, and degradation of the Aboriginal peoples. . .The present

plight, in terms of health, employment, education, living conditions and self-esteem, of so many Aborigines must be acknowledged as largely flowing from what happened in the past. The dispossession, the destruction of hunting fields and the devastation of lives were all related. The new diseases, the alcohol and the new pressures of living were all introduced.

A sincere, unequivocal acknowledgment and apology to Aboriginal peoples for past injustices by our national and state governments, on behalf of all Australian people, is clearly a necessary first step in the healing process of this blight in Australia's history.

A significant and complex factor in the dispossession of Aboriginal people is the role played by the missions. Christian missionaries of various denominations travelled to both accessible and remote regions of the country, creating settlements with a view to converting traditional Aboriginal peoples from their indigenous spiritual beliefs to the imported religious systems. Some missionaries were more sensitive than others, incorporating Aboriginal beliefs into a Christian framework, while others demanded that Aboriginal peoples abandon their 'pagan' beliefs and languages altogether. Many of the early missionaries imposed their western cultural values quite vigorously, endeavouring to suppress Aboriginal spiritual beliefs and ritual practices by banning all forms of traditional song and dance, in themselves essential expressions of Aboriginal spirituality. In some missions children were separated from their parents and then trained as unpaid servants or manual labourers. This prevented parents from passing on to their children traditional Aboriginal spiritual knowledge and beliefs.

Most Christian missions were appointed by government departments as agencies through which to channel and administer education and medical supplies, and this gave government-endorsed missions widespread control over the lives of many Aboriginal people. While it is certainly true that a number of missionaries helped Aboriginal people acquire skills valued by white society, especially at such settlements as New Norcia in Western Australia and Hermannsburg in the Northern Territory, it remains evident that in relation to the endeavours of the missionaries across the country the number of Christian conversions were relatively few.

Nevertheless, today many Aboriginal people value, and have incorporated, their understanding of Christianity into their Dreamtime cosmology in ways that for them are positive and complementary. As Noel Wallace has observed, among the Pitjantjatjara people at Ernabella Mission, for example, it was often possible to reconcile traditional spiritual concepts with Christianity because the latter was accepted as 'whitefella Dreaming', and for some Aboriginal Christians 'God must have made the Spirit Ancestors because He made everything'. Another Aboriginal group has developed this religious syncretism into what they call 'The Rainbow Spirit Theology' — a theology which honours the Rainbow Serpent as the Creator. Other groups are also working towards developing syncretic theologies that they hope will reflect a uniquely Australian spirituality. However, there can also be a sinister aspect to religious conversion. An example of this is the urban evangelical movement derived from the Aboriginal Evangelical Fellowship, which was originally known as Mama Kurunpa ('Father Spirit') but subsequently retitled Mama Garum'pa by Europeans and Aboriginal people who no longer speak their native dialects.

This evangelical Christian sect is now registered as a mining company, and claims that Jesus gave the country to all people, not just Aborigines, so that land rights for Aboriginal people are irrelevant. The political and economic motives of religious organisations of this sort are obvious.[4]

One of the most contentious issues in Australian history has been the concept of terra nullius — the idea of a land over which no previous sovereignty has been exercised. In relation to the Australian continent, the doctrine of terra nullius commenced with James Cook's claim in 1770 to eastern Australia and culminated with Charles Fremantle's annexation of western Australia in 1829. This concept, although based on a legal fiction, was not tested legally until the first 'native title' case in 1970, which arose over a dispute between traditional Yirrkala Aboriginal landholders and the Nabalco Mining Company. Here Justice Blackburn, presiding in the Northern Territory Supreme Court, found that the traditional cultural and religious links between Yirrkala's Yolngu people and the land did not represent a 'proprietary interest' in the land — a judgment which in effect affirmed the official government policy that Australia was 'no one's land' prior to white occupation and that theoretically Yirrkala had become subject to British law from 1788 onwards. A major petition in the form of a bark painting, an appropriate cultural expression, had earlier been presented by the Yolngu people of the Yirrkala community in the Federal Parliament. This historically significant 1963 bark petition, signed by seventeen Yolngu elders, remains on display at Parliament House in Canberra.

In a 'landmark' law of 1976, the *Aboriginal Land Rights (Northern Territory) Act* (ALRA) was passed by the Federal Parliament — some 482,868 square kilometres (299,861 square miles), approximately 36 per cent of the Northern Territory, was returned to Aboriginal ownership under freehold title. During this case, and in subsequent land claim hearings (such as that of the Utopia Pastoral Lease in 1979)[5], Aboriginal Law women and men from several communities gave evidence in the traditional ceremonial forms. In so doing these Aboriginal people demonstrated extensive and intimate knowledge of their country. The Utopia community in Central Australia regained freehold title to traditional clan lands in 1979 under the *ALRA Act* of 1976. However, successful Aboriginal land rights claims, such as those in the Northern Territory, have not resolved the more complicated 'native title' issues related to Aboriginal people as a whole.

Australia's most prominent native title case, *Mabo v State of Queensland (No 2)* in 1992, was argued in the High Court within the context of the *Racial Discrimination Act* and overruled Justice Blackburn's earlier decision. The Mabo judgment held that Australia was not terra nullius; that Australian sovereignty was derivative, having changed in 1788 from prior Aboriginal sovereignty, and that British common law, introduced with settlement, coexisted with prior Aboriginal and Torres Strait Islander laws of land ownership, which, until extinguished, survived the change in sovereignty and that native title was a common law right. As a consequence, it was held that Australian courts must recognise Aboriginal rights to land — that is, native title. This native title case was named after Koiki (Eddie) Mabo (1937-92) who had been born on Mer (Murray Island) in the Torres Strait. Mabo was the first named plaintiff in this land rights action, which he and four other Torres Strait Islanders brought before the Queensland Supreme Court and the High Court of Australia which brought down the judgment. Eddie Mabo died of cancer four months before the High Court delivered its findings.

A further development of vital concern to the issue of native title is now widely known as the 'Wik judgment'. The Wik peoples, who are said to be among the most traditional of Queensland Aboriginal peoples despite Christian infiltration into their traditional belief systems, live on Cape York Peninsula and have vigorously campaigned against the mining industry and the land practices of various Queensland governments. 'Wik' is a term which refers collectively to a number of Aboriginal groups (such as the Wik-Mungkana, the Wik-Thinta, the Wik-Nganychara among others) who occupy land between Weipa and Pormpuraaw on western Cape York Peninsula, from the Archer River to near the Edward River and inland to the centre of the Cape. In December 1996, in a response to actions brought by the Wik peoples, the High Court ruled that pastoral leases did not necessarily extinguish native title and that native title could coexist with pastoral leases but that pastoral rights would prevail in the case of conflict. This ruling has been controversial since its inception. Considerable and very vocal opposition has developed between the affected parties, and there has been much ongoing political activism and lobbying surrounding its implications by federal and state governments, Aboriginal councils, pastoralists, local and international media. At the time of writing, the consequences of the Wik decision have not been fully resolved. The present prime minister has proposed a 'Ten Point Plan' to his Liberal/National Party coalition government which overrides the Wik decision and effectively, though not explicitly, eradicates native title to land at present tenanted by white pastoralists. The legal ramifications of the prime minister's proposal are complex and have many ongoing consequences.

Clearly underlying much of this dispute, however, is the continuing and fundamental issue of reconciliation — for historically there is a need for Aboriginal and non-Aboriginal peoples to live together in a climate of mutual respect and tolerance. With this issue in mind, in December 1991 a council of 25 members, comprising twelve Aboriginal people, two Torres Strait Islanders and eleven other Australians was appointed, with Aboriginal leader Patrick Dodson as its first chairperson. This was the culmination of a process launched in September 1991 with the passage of an Act, passed unanimously by both houses of parliament, to formally guide the reconciliation process. At its first meeting in Canberra in February 1992, the council agreed on a vision of Australian society for 2001: a united Australia which would respect this land, value Aboriginal and Torres Strait Islander heritage, and provide justice and equity for all. The council identified eight key issues for reconciliation, including: achieving a greater understanding of the land and sea in Aboriginal and Torres Strait Islander society; promoting a greater awareness of the causes of disadvantage that prevent Aboriginal and Torres Strait Islander peoples from achieving fair and proper standards in health, housing, employment and education; and agreeing on whether the process of reconciliation would be advanced by a document of reconciliation.

Speaking at the first national conference on Aboriginal reconciliation, in Victoria this year (1997), Patrick Dodson emphasised that the quest for reconciliation must now become a priority for all Australians: 'All the wisdom and love here will provide tools in the fight for true reconciliation. . . all the pains in the battle are nothing when the goal is just and honourable.' The delegates' closing address, A Call to the Nation, included these statements:

We, the participants at this convention, affirm to all the people of this nation that reconciliation between Australia's indigenous peoples and other Australians is central to the renewal of this nation as a harmonious and just society which lives out its national ethos of a fair go for all; and that until we achieve such reconciliation this nation will remain diminished. . .We call on our fellow Australians to join together across this land to build a people's movement for reconciliation of sufficient breadth and power to guarantee that Australia can truly celebrate the centenary of its nationhood in 2001, confident that it has established a sound foundation for reconciliation. . .This will ensure that Australians can walk together beyond the centenary of Federation into the next millennium towards the vision of a united Australia which respects this land of ours, values the Aboriginal and Torres Strait Islander heritage and provides justice and equity for all.

With the exception of the recent debate over the Wik decision, perhaps the most provocative event of recent times has been the bicentennial celebration of 1988, which, by celebrating 200 years of white settlement and largely ignoring Australia's Aboriginal history, marshalled formerly discrete Aboriginal groups into a united protest against their treatment by the British since Australia's colonisation. This extraordinary insensitivity to Aboriginal history — a history vastly different to white history — led to 'Australia Day' being named 'Invasion Day' or 'Survival Day' (their 'Day of Mourning') by Aboriginal groups and the 'celebration' was marked by mass protests in Sydney.

Nevertheless there have been positive outcomes of reconciliation already, such as the 1996 Cape York Regional Agreement, and the spirit of mutual respect will hopefully emerge in the wake of the Wik judgment, despite current conflicts. In 1980, for example, internationally known tribal elder of the Yuin people of Wallaga Lake in New South Wales, Guboo (Good Friend) Ted Thomas, began the 'Renewing the Dreaming' camps in land alienated from Aboriginal culture. These annual gatherings, initiated at Goolaga (Mount Dromedary) on the South Coast of New South Wales, are committed to re-awakening the Dreaming in the hearts and minds of those openly willing to learn, and are particularly oriented towards the younger generations as future spiritual leaders and custodians of the land and their cultural heritage. Acutely aware of the spiritual and ecological plight of present generations of Aboriginal people, Guboo fought a successful campaign in 1979 to preserve Mumballa Mountain,[6] which contains many Yuin sacred sites, from the damage wrought by the wood-chipping industry. This action sowed the seeds for the first land rights settlement for Aboriginal peoples in New South Wales. Guboo emerged from this 1979 campaign as a restorer of the sacredness of sites desecrated through so-called 'development' and has travelled widely to meet and learn from the spiritual elders of other indigenous nations. Guboo has said: 'Now we need people throughout this nation to accept custodianship for areas of land in their locality and prepare these places for a restoration of their Dreaming so that energies flow out to affect the vegetative, sentient and human spheres.'

At this stage, says Guboo, 'the Renewing of the Dreaming is defined in this way:

Renewing the Dreaming is the re-establishment of our innate spiritual relationship with the Earth, using as a starting point the sources of power at selected sites. It is a

movement toward reviving identity with the natural environment for the birth of a
truly Australian culture. Its aims are: to bring into ourselves and into our culture the
power latent within centres of consciousness and energy in the natural environment;
to forge links with Aboriginal ancestors, people and culture; to encourage
identification, recording, preservation and use of specific sites; to support land rights
and reparations for Aboriginal people; to develop appreciation and understanding of
environment protection. . .; to formulate a Dreaming Wisdom appropriate to the
contemporary way of life.'[7]

In order for a true process of spiritual renewal and reconciliation to occur between Aboriginal
and non-Aboriginal peoples, it is vital for us as a nation to attempt to understand our collective
and individual history, in order to know how we have arrived — and with what baggage —
into the present. This journey encompasses acknowledging the darkness in both our country's
and our own biographies, as well as applauding our achievements. It is important that we see
this as an inner journey as well as an external one so that we can detect and address the seeds
of racism, the inequities, the fear of difference and the unknown within ourselves and ask why
we continue to wreak devastation on the land — our Mother and the life-support system that
sustains us all. Only then can we address these issues in the wider cultural context with any
wisdom and confidence, and seek to achieve lasting resolutions to historical conflicts which
continue on in the lives of present generations.

We as a nation, and as individuals, need to reacquaint ourselves with the stories of this
land, and not simply the Eurocentric or Anglo-Celtic versions that began 200 years ago. We
need to attempt to understand — from what is recorded, from Aboriginal people, from our
own powers of imagining — the astonishing history of this ancient continent and the
mythological or spiritual wealth of its Aboriginal inhabitants. This book is a small offering to
that end, in exploring some aspects of the vast Dreamtime mythology and relationships that
link Aboriginal cultures spiritually to the land. Aboriginal peoples have struggled hard and
endured much adversity to eventually have their history and their unique identity
acknowledged and accepted. They are willing to share their stories and their vast knowledge
about this country if only we will listen, and they have waited a long time to be asked. Up and
down the country Aboriginal people say that 'White man got no Dreaming.' Muta, a Murinbara
man who first used the phrase 'White man got no Dreaming' expressed this observation as
follows:

White man got no Dreaming,
White man, him go 'nother way.
White man, him go different.
Him got road belong himself.[8]

By this is meant that 'white' peoples have no sustaining and binding spiritual vision — either
between each other or between themselves and the land. Aboriginal peoples know that such
a vision and way of living is essential for individual, social and ecological health.

Non-Aboriginal people cannot, and need not, adopt Aboriginal spirituality as their own,
but as all human beings are bound by one Earth, there is much that the accumulated wisdom

of the Dreamtime legacy — what we are calling 'wisdom from the Earth' — can teach us all. In western culture's drive to 'possess' and unremittingly 'develop', to attempt to control Nature, to economically rationalise human and other life, to oppress indigenous peoples and other cultural minorities, much valuable knowledge and wisdom has been lost or forgotten. We need to understand the value of what we have lost as well as what we have gained in the name of 'development'. Perhaps then it may be possible to retrieve what is needed for the land and the people to live in harmony once again, in ways that embrace contemporary and ancient understandings. It appears to be a critical time for us to acknowledge our collective inheritances, both positive and negative, to claim our independence and to responsibly come to terms with the past as best we may so that we can move into the future as a basically united, though diverse, nation. A nation bound by one land with many roots, a nation that offers hope for the dreams of future generations.

It has been said that crisis is also opportunity. Although there currently appears to be yet another crisis between the clashing world views of 'black' and 'white' Australians, let us hope that this is a dark hour before a new dawn of understanding. This book endeavours to sound a note of celebration, amidst the pain and the healing of these testing times, for the extraordinary beauty and cultural richness that characterises this land.

Nganyinytja, a tribal elder and initiate of the elder's Law of the Pitjantjatjara Aboriginal people of Central Australia and co-partner with her husband Ilyatjari, of the Angatja Bush College, extends an invitation to us all:

Ngalya pitja ngayuku ngura nyakuntjikitja. Manta nyangatja milmilpatjara! Ngayuku kamiku tjamuku ngura iritinguru. Pitjaya! Pina ala, kuru ala, kututu alatjara!

Come and see my country. This land is sacred! This has been my grandmother's and grandfather's country from a long time ago. Come with open ears, open eyes and an open heart.[9]

And so it is that we now begin at the Beginning. . .

Inside the earth lives — today and always — Wunggud, a big snake.

She is the earth and of the primeval substance from which everything in Nature

is formed. She is female, njindi, *'her'. Before Creation, she was tightly coiled into*

a ball of jelly-like substance, ngallalla yawun, *'everything soft like jelly'.*

Wunggud is the Earth Snake, the name, body, substance and power of the earth.

All of nature grows on the body of the Snake.[1]

Chapter One

CREATION

All cultures have their myths[2], or religious beliefs, about Creation, about Beginnings, about how the World came into being. The majestic time of Creation in Aboriginal Australia, when the Ancestor Spirits formed, named and breathed life and language into all that exists in the known Universe — the plants, animals, elements, celestial bodies, humans and social organisation — is the touchstone of all Aboriginal cultural and religious practice. It is this divine inheritance — known as the Law — that has always been, and is, continuously re-enacted as it was in the first times by Aboriginal peoples throughout the Australian continent.

Ceremonial activities performed at the sacred sites of their Spirit Ancestors are integral to Aboriginal identity and relationship, and their sense of responsibility in the continuation of all species. In Aboriginal cosmology, everything and everybody, all space and all time, is intertwined and interdependent, and all are kin. Aboriginal peoples recognise that they have a spark of their Spirit Ancestors within them, which can be activated in ceremony and ritual, and thus they have an unbroken link to the Creation Epoch, known in English as the eternal 'Dreamtime' or the 'Dreaming'. This essence of the Spirit Ancestors — held as a life force within them, as well as in all features and creatures of the sacred Earth and the Cosmos — gives Aboriginal peoples the primal awareness that they are an integral aspect of primordial Creation, and thus are part of all that ever was and ever will be. It is this knowledge that they revere and celebrate: the dawn of today is in essence the same as the dawn of the Universe.

In most cultures, peoples have asked the eternal questions about who we are, why we are alive today, and what our purpose is on this Earth. It is these questions, and the answers that arise in response to them, that give our lives meaning. Traditional Aboriginal peoples seem to have no need of these questions in a philosophical sense; they know who they are and where they came from because they accept as absolute truth the events of the Dreamtime and the myths or stories of the actions and bequests of their Spirit Ancestors. In modern western cultures, the concepts of an innate spirituality, holistic values and mythic reality as integral dimensions of human life have been replaced by secular and reductionist materialism.

At this time of global ecological crisis, there is much that indigenous peoples the World over can teach us, for their spiritual traditions invariably reflect a deep and profound bond

Opposite: *The Beginning of Time* by Paddy Fordham Wainbarrnga, a Rembarrnga man from central Arnhem Land, Northern Territory. This image depicts the Beginning of Life itself. The revered and feared Bolong (Rainbow Serpent) is recognised by Aboriginal tribes around Australia as being the Creator of Life. When the Bolong (who has female and male aspects) created life, s/he placed all living things into categories or moieties — in Arnhem Land these are *Dua* and *Yirritja* (or *Jiritja*). Aboriginal people recognise that it is the continued cycle in Life between *Dua* and *Yirritja* which provides the meaning of existence itself. Courtesy of Coo-ee Aboriginal Art.

*Bandaiyan —
body of Australia —
as drawn by David Mowaljarlai,
Ngarinyin Law man of the
Kimberley, Western Australia.
Courtesy of Jutta Malnic.*

with the Earth. These traditions also embody an intimate knowledge, accumulated over millennia, of the workings of the natural world. It is out of their love and deep concern for the Earth and her species that indigenous peoples are now willing to share their profound knowledge and ancient wisdom. Native groups everywhere — including Australian Aboriginal peoples — acknowledge that in order for the Earth and all beings who depend on her to survive into the future, a deeply respectful and reciprocal approach to the environment is now critical. They recognise that the World was shaped by forces much greater than humankind, and will continue long after we have each departed this planet.

Regardless of cultural variations, Creation myths in all regions of the World endeavour to explain how the Universe came into existence, and describe the ways in which humans, animals and plants were first conceived. These myths also throw light on the relationship between the founding deities — the Goddesses, Gods and Ancestral Spirits of Creation — and those created beings, ourselves included, who marvel in response to all they find around them. Myths invariably evoke a sense of awe because they are dealing with great and profound mysteries. They are describing how tangible 'realities' emerged from formlessness and chaos, how things of great beauty and worth came into the World. These stories deal with ultimate meaning and strike at the very fabric of our existence.

For all Aboriginal peoples, the monumental events of the Creation epic — the 'Dreamtime' — are the defining and eternal moment, for it was at this time that the Spirit Ancestors first roamed the face of the Earth, shaping and naming the World through their mighty actions and spiritual power, and creating all that was true and valuable.

According to Aboriginal tradition, the World did not simply emerge mysteriously from nothingness or the 'big bang' of scientific theory. Before the World came into existence, there was a mass of dark and formless matter, conceived of variously by different tribal groups as a vast watery expanse or as a somewhat featureless plain. It was not so much that the World was created out of nothing, rather that the Spirit Ancestors defined all spaces and all time out of what was potentially there in this dark, nameless matter — what elder David Mowaljarlai, of the Ngarinyin people of the Kimberley region, calls *ngallalla yawun,* 'everything soft like jelly'. The Spirit Ancestors lay deep beneath the surface of this shapeless and nameless World, then emerged to create the forms and identities of the many plants and animals that are now recognised as totemic species. Spirit Ancestors also came from the sky, and they too performed their deeds and returned to the heavens. And so it was at this time that the Spirit Ancestors came forth as Rainbow Serpent Women, Kangaroo Men, Sisters from the Sky, Bush Fig Men or

Mulga Seed Women, and so on in a myriad array of different identities. These Spirit Ancestors became the prototypes of all creatures who are alive today and at the same time established a line of descendants linked to what are now living representatives of those plant and animal forms. The Dreamtime myths recount these events in profound poetic beauty.

THE ETERNAL DREAMTIME

The eternal 'Dreamtime' or the 'Dreaming' is an English concept which is referred to by different names by Aboriginal peoples according to the language of their regional group. For the Pitjantjatjara of north-west South Australia this celebrated sacred time of Creation is known as *Tjukurrpa* or *Tjugurba*; for the Arrernte (or Aranda) of Central Australia — who prefer the term 'Time of Great Power' — it is *Altyerre*, *Altjeringa*, *Alcheringa* or *Aldjerinya*; for the Yolngu people of north-east Arnhem Land it is *Wongar* or *Wangarr*; to the Kukatja people of Western Australia it is *Ngarangkarni*; and to the Ngarinyin people of the Kimberley region of Western Australia it is *Lalai*. To Aboriginal peoples, regardless of regional group affiliation, these terms have meaning far greater than the words Dreamtime or Dreaming imply — a meaning more akin to the quintessence of existence itself and which encompasses the land and the people.

Unlike other religious traditions which celebrate at separate times to everyday life a

revelatory event in the long distant past, the Dreamtime of Aboriginal spiritual practice is celebrated and lives in whatever exists and transpires in the present — in all aspects of Creation, in an eternal now. In this sense all time exists in the present moment and all life — the Spirit Ancestors, the Earth, the Cosmos and all species — are aspects of an inherited divine order and are thus sacramental. There is no 'thing' in Aboriginal consciousness that is 'nothing'. There is no aspect, no creature — be it a dung beetle, a poisonous snake or a human being — that does not have its place and its role to play in the ordained sacred pattern of Creation. There are no gods, no religious hierarchies, no segregation of 'good' and 'bad', no unsavoury bits, and no separation between the physical and the spiritual or nature, humanity and culture. All came into being at the one time, and all of these dimensions are reflections of each other.

The Dreamtime that encodes the exploits of the Spirit Ancestors, while located in the Creation of the past, is also embodied in the present — in the land and in the Aboriginal descendants of those original Beings. In this way, the Dreamtime encompasses past reality and future possibilities in an eternally sacred present. Thus all of Creation and all Time are contained in a diverse multiplicity of one sacred reality. Irrespective of the particular names ascribed to it, the Dreamtime holds the idea that all aspects of life are eternally interconnected in a vast web of relationship, for all creatures and all things have their origin in the sacred events of the Creation.

The Creation journeys of the Spirit Ancestors are both a metaphysical and geographical mapping of the Australian continent. The events which transpired during this extraordinary Epoch are contained in the vast living body of myth that constitutes the eternal Dreamtime — mythic stories which have been orally transmitted by teaching stories, song, dance, art, ritual and ceremony to countless generations of Aboriginal peoples to the present day.

While there are regional differences in the Dreamtime song line stories, one pervasive myth, and perhaps the most important deity in Aboriginal Australia, is the creative and destructive, usually female, Rainbow Serpent — who slumbered beneath the ground and then pushed through to the surface, writhing across the land and giving form to the distinctive topographical features which are recognised today. Other Creation myths recount how Ancestor Spirits rose up from the sea, and then in turn came onto the land, creating everything that exists, while other legends tell how Sky-beings descended from the stars and returned to different regions of the heavens.

These Spirit Beings not only made everything, but they also gave plants and animals their names and distinctive markings. They created the sacred teachings of the Dreaming — the Law — they established customs, they taught humans how to hunt, how to utilise fire and make cooking utensils, how to dance and perform ceremonies, and they invented languages so that different tribal groups could communicate with each other. Later, after the Dreamtime Ancestors completed their tasks, they grew weary and returned once more to a state of slumber. As the Ancestors could change their shape, some disappeared back into the Earth, some transformed themselves into distinctive features within the landscape — becoming sacred mountains, waterholes, markings on rocks and cliff-faces, fissures in the ground and so on — while others returned to the sky. As a legacy, some of them left spirit children behind in waterholes, and these spirit children could then enter pregnant females and be born as a manifestation of the Spirit Ancestor.

However, even though the Spirit Ancestors withdrew from their specific roles in the Creation process and were hidden from view, this did not mean that they were no longer alive, conscious and powerful. In Aboriginal spiritual tradition, the force of the Spirit Ancestor resides at the location of their resting place, and this spiritual power can be tapped through ritual by those who understand how to use this power. These sacred sites are consecrated ground and thus have profound significance for Aboriginal people. The activities of the Creation Epoch

provided the pattern for how life should be lived for all time, and there is a profound recognition of this concept within the rich ceremonial life of Aboriginal peoples.

Ceremonies and rituals reflect on all aspects of daily life — from hunting and gathering food and health and healing practices, through to how to look after 'country' and the metaphysics of birth, initiation and death — and provide ritual recognition of the different phases of human development. At the same time, the Dreamtime myths provide guidance on recurrent human experiences — like pleasure and pain, sexuality, grief and suffering, the quest for food, shelter and safety, and the transition from youth to old age — and they provide a basis for appropriate behaviour, with its attendant rewards and punishments. However, the Dreamtime Epoch is not an idealised concept among Aboriginal peoples, and their Spirit Ancestors loved, hunted, fought, killed, envied, ate, danced, had intercourse, struggled, died and at times transgressed the Law in the same ways as their descendants. The Ancestor Spirits were seen to be inherently both 'good' and 'bad', just like their Aboriginal descendants.

Many Aboriginal myths relate conflict situations and, by way of illustrating qualities which led to conflict — such as betrayal, violence and lust — they highlight outcomes which provide both explanations of how things came about and clarification of potentially threatening areas not to be taken for granted. The Creation narratives rarely moralise, however, about the rights and wrongs of what an Ancestor figure did or did not do — in the Dreamtime myths the Ancestors do not sit in judgment or promise salvation in Heaven. Often the stories invite the listener to form her or his own judgment about whether an outcome was justified or not, though the outcome itself is rarely questioned. The emphasis in the mythic legacy is more one of personal and collective responsibility.

There can be no doubt that the myths of the Dreamtime provide blueprints and a cumulative body of knowledge that link all Aboriginal peoples with the events of the Creation. These include, for example, instructions on how to make fire, rituals for fire ceremonies and rainmaking, customs on initiations and behaviour to be adhered to in marriage and other social practices, such as in death and mortuary ceremonies, and rituals to look after land. It is this inheritance that is, and always has been, continuously re-enacted and celebrated by Aborigines across the continent. These ceremonial activities encompass all aspects of Aboriginal identity, and provide not only a sense of connection and relationship but also an awareness of the continuity and interconnectedness of all forms of being.

Individual performers may imitate the form of specific Dreamtime Ancestors — like a goanna, kangaroo, emu or serpent, for example — and 'dance' these beings to the accompaniment of *didjeridus* and rhythmic wooden clapsticks. In so doing they are not simply playing a role but ritually 'become' that Ancestor Spirit. Similarly, for an Aboriginal mother a birth which occurs today as a literal and personal experience is also an archetypal event linked to the mythic birth of the World. In carrying out ascribed responsibilities to the land and to all kin, Aboriginal peoples honour their connection with the Ancestors and preserve their culture for future generations.

In a very specific way the Creation myths provide an account of how things have come to be. It may be that the place where a Kangaroo Ancestor thumped his tail on the ground is now a limestone outcrop, or that the native cat now has spots on its body because its Dreamtime Ancestor got sores on its skin. Perhaps an Ancestor who sat up and surveyed the country later became a rocky ridge, the winding track of a serpent became a watercourse, a bush shelter constructed by a group of sisters became a cave, or bush tomatoes gathered by a group of women later became a cluster of small stones. Similarly, for many Aboriginal people there are specific associations of species and place: the goanna is often linked with sandy outcrops, the kingfisher with coal, and the crested pigeon with grinding stones. The stories when told in a secular manner out of context, however, assume a different meaning. The stories of the Dreamtime are not simple legends or fables, nor are they like the mythology of the Greeks, Scandinavians or the Ancient Egyptians. The Dreamtime stories comprise a living mythology depicting actual events linked to specific geographical sites which create a vast, sophisticated, cohesive and connected series of maps of the entire Australian land. To an Aboriginal person trained in traditional Law, the entire continent reveals signposts of meaning.

DREAMTIME AND DREAMINGS

It is important to distinguish between the Dreamtime of the Creation Epoch and specific Dreamings which are linked to specific regions of land and become the custodial responsibility of certain Aboriginal people. The words 'Dreamtime' and 'Dreamings' are themselves problematical, the first apparently having been coined by the explorers Baldwin Spencer and F. J. Gillen in the early part of this century, and the latter more recently proposed by the anthropologist W. E. H. Stanner. Some Aboriginal people do use the phrases 'Dreamtime' and 'Dreaming' when they are attempting to communicate their concepts in English, but there is a certain awkwardness in these terms. The Arrernte term *altjiranga ngambakala* has the inference of 'having originated out of one's own eternity', 'immortal', 'uncreated', and it is this which is essential to the concept of the Dreamtime or the Dreaming. At the same time, *altji rarma* means 'to see or dream eternal things', or 'to see with eternal vision'.[3]

Some westerners could mistakenly assume that for Aboriginal peoples the Dreamtime has the same relationship to the everyday world that dreams do in relation to our conscious waking perception — namely that one realm is a world of 'fantasy' imagery, while the other is grounded in material 'reality'. This type of distinction is clearly not applicable if we are to appreciate the underlying concepts of the Aboriginal spiritual tradition, although it is certainly true in Aboriginal culture that through dreams and visions individuals may make contact with the Spirit Ancestors and in this way receive sacred information.

The concept of the Dreamtime recalls a majestic and sacred time in the remote past when the Spirit Ancestors came upon the Earth to create the exquisite waterholes, beautiful caves and mountains of a sacred landscape, and to provide an abundant resource of plants and animals for sustenance. However, for Aboriginal peoples, the Dreaming also continues today: it is the bond between that eternal moment of Creation and the particular area of land, or the specific totemic plants and animals, which symbolise the vital link with the Beginning.

When Aboriginal artists paint their Dreaming they are producing a map of their 'country' — a map of their own spiritual and earthly terrain — and each artist is intimately acquainted with the journeys and exploits of their Spirit Ancestors and totem animals which unfolded as part of the Dreamtime saga. In this sense, the Ancestor Spirits are thus symbolised in the Dreamings and, in a metaphysical sense, are the Dreamings, and as such have both preceded and continue to exist in present-day generations. So a Dreaming terrain

is both one of the land and the spirit, for the two are one and the same. The land is alive, the rocks and trees are alive, the plants are alive — the World is pervaded by the spirit of the Founding Ancestors and this sense of an overriding 'oneness' provides a guiding model for how one should live one's life: in a state of attunement and harmony with how things have always been since the Beginning.

The Spirit Ancestors of the Dreaming provided the foundation model for life. They established a pattern for the daily round of cultural practices known as the Law — whether this related to social, economic, political or ritual activities. All of the ways that people behave and relate to each other — hunting, sharing food, having sexual relations, making tools and other objects, in land ceremonies, singing songs, drawing symbolic designs, punishing wrongdoers — are the way they are because the Spirit Ancestors behaved in these ways too.

Aboriginal peoples believe, without doubt, that the Spirit Ancestors left these behavioural examples to be followed. The Dreamtime myths reflect the daily events in the lives of the people of particular regions, and just as Aboriginal peoples depended on hunting, fishing and gathering food for daily sustenance, similarly the Spirit Ancestors are depicted as engaging in these pursuits in the Dreaming. Even in the most mundane tasks, people relive the events of the Dreaming. The particular roles of females and males, the ways that food was prepared, cooked and shared, the use of implements — all of these were pre-ordained by the Ancestors. Thus Aboriginal peoples at all times live in a sanctified Universe — there are only degrees of sacred living, with the mundane at one end of the spectrum and secret–sacred ritual and ceremonial enactment at the other, but all activity is held with the knowledge that all aspects of life are a manifestation and reflection of the one Divine Reality.

Eddie Kneebone offers a perceptive insight into the spiritual link between the Dreamtime, the land and each individual human being:

> Aboriginal spirituality is the belief and the feeling within yourself that allows you to become part of the whole environment around you — not the built environment, but the natural environment. . .Birth, life and death are all part of it, and you welcome each.
>
> Aboriginal spirituality is the belief that the soul or spirit will continue on after our physical form has passed away through death. The spirit will return to the Dreamtime from where it came, it will carry our memories to the Dreamtime and eventually it will return again through birth, either as a human or an animal or even trees and rocks. The shape is not important because everything is equal and shares the same soul or spirit from the Dreamtime.[4]

The bond each individual feels with the Ancestors of the Dreamtime is very tangible. As Mudrooroo writes in his book *Aboriginal Mythology*:

> The creative period of the 'Dreamtime' is as much metaphysical as an epoch in time. Aboriginal people can bring into present the *djang*, the spiritual energy of those times, by engaging in rituals which the ancestors taught and connecting up with them. They believe that the spark of life, the soul which energises them, is part of that ancestor, so that by stimulating that part through ritual and ceremony a breakthrough can be made into the timeless time of the 'Dreaming', when all things are made and continue to be made.[5]

THE RAINBOW SERPENT

When one considers the Creation Epoch and the monumental drama of the Dreamtime, one is bound also to consider the Rainbow Serpent, which is perhaps the most significant Creator Being in Aboriginal mythology. In different contexts the Rainbow Creator has both female and male characteristics, but is usually considered female — a sacred embodiment of the Earth. She is associated both with rocks and waterholes and is the Ancestor of all forms of life, the Mother of all Being.

The distinguished Aboriginal poet Oodgeroo (Kath Walker) of the tribe Noonuccal, was a custodian of the island of Minjerribah in Moreton Bay, near Brisbane. Towards the end of her long and eventful life, she expounded her spiritual beliefs in a staged performance at the

Brisbane Expo of 1988. This was *The Rainbow Serpent*, which she composed with the help of her son, Kabul. In the play an indigenous elder says:

> We are different you and me. We say that the earth is our mother
> — we cannot own her, she own us. . .

> This rock and all these rocks are alive with her spirit. They protect us, all of us.
> They are her, what you fullas say now, temple. . .

> Since the *Alcheringa,* that thing
> you fulla call Dreamtime, this place has
> given man shelter from the heat, a place
> to paint, to dance the sacred dance and
> talk to his spirit.

> How does one repay such gifts?

> By protecting the land.

> [In the play, the deity appears and the elder introduces Oodgeroo's totem,
> or Dreaming:]

> This is my totem, Kabul. You know her as the Carpet Snake. She my tribe's symbol of the
> Rainbow Serpent, the giver and taker of life. Sometimes she is called Borlung, sometimes
> Ngalyod. She has many names, that wise one.

> Belief in this snake deity is spread all across Australia. It is connected with many things
> including magic. Many of her ceremonies and rituals are a secret beyond a secret and are
> not to be disclosed except to an initiate of equal status, though she may also be a
> personal and tribal totem.

> [So Oodgeroo summons the Dreamtime:]

> In the time of *Alcheringa*, the land lay flat and cold. The world, she empty. The Rainbow
> Serpent, she asleep under the ground with all the animal tribes in her belly waiting to
> be born. When it her time, she push up.[6]

This breaking through of the Spirit into form is a theme found in many of the World's mythologies. In encountering Aboriginal spirituality one is introduced to the idea of a vast sacred territory, created and shaped by Spirit Ancestors who leave their indelible imprint upon the landscape and who also provide a code for living one's life upon the Earth. All across Aboriginal Australia one is able to find more localised Creation myths which describe the activities of Spirit Ancestors in different parts of the terrain. These evocative accounts reinforce the living reality of the Creation Epoch and are collectively the mythology of the eternal Dreamtime.

In contemporary western cultures the word 'myth' has come to mean fantasy, lie or erroneous belief. This is a reversal of its original meaning. Myths were and are the spiritual beliefs underpinning religious practices of many world cultures. Joseph Campbell, the eminent geographer of comparative mythology, suggests that myths are the collective

Ngalyod (the Rainbow Serpent) by Gunbalanya (Oenpelli) artist Djawida of the Gunwinggu (or Kunwinjku) people. Ngalyod is much feared by Aboriginal people living at Gunbalanya in the Northern Territory. He sleeps during the dry season in fresh water billabongs in the escarpment country and when it is time for the wet season to begin, Ngalyod leaves his resting place and goes up into the sky. The vapour from his breath forms storm clouds, and loud growls from his mouth roll across the sky making thunder. The artist, Djawida, shows Ngalyod with the head of a crocodile with a feathered headdress, the body of a python and the barbs of a crocodile along a pointed tail. Ngalyod's face can resemble that of a kangaroo, a crocodile or some other creature. He is often depicted with a feathered headdress like those worn by Aboriginal people in ceremonies honouring Ngalyod. Courtesy of Coo-ee Aboriginal Art.

dreams of a culture. Myths fundamentally reside in mystery as they relate to expressions of Divine Reality and cannot really be pinned down as they change their divine notions over time.

The following accounts of Dreamtime myths provide a glimpse into this mythic/spiritual heritage, though Aboriginal Creation stories emanate from an oral tradition and are always contextualised in *relationship* to the land and to particular people. Also, there are many layers to the traditional expression of a myth, in sign, symbol and metaphor, in oral story-telling, in song, dance, art and ritual. There are also initiatory considerations in Dreaming myths or 'inside/outside' stories as they are also called — 'inside' referring to secret-sacred knowledge and purposes only to be revealed to initiates and 'outside' meaning able to be revealed to the uninitiated or to outsiders. Attempting to capture a spoken myth, or Creation song, in a one-dimensional and abbreviated written form can only indicate the richness of this cultural world view, and cannot convey the re-creation process involved in the personal transmission of myth from one generation to another. The process of oral culture serves to maintain the *living* dynamic of cultural knowledge rather than freezing information in time, which is what happens in the written story form.

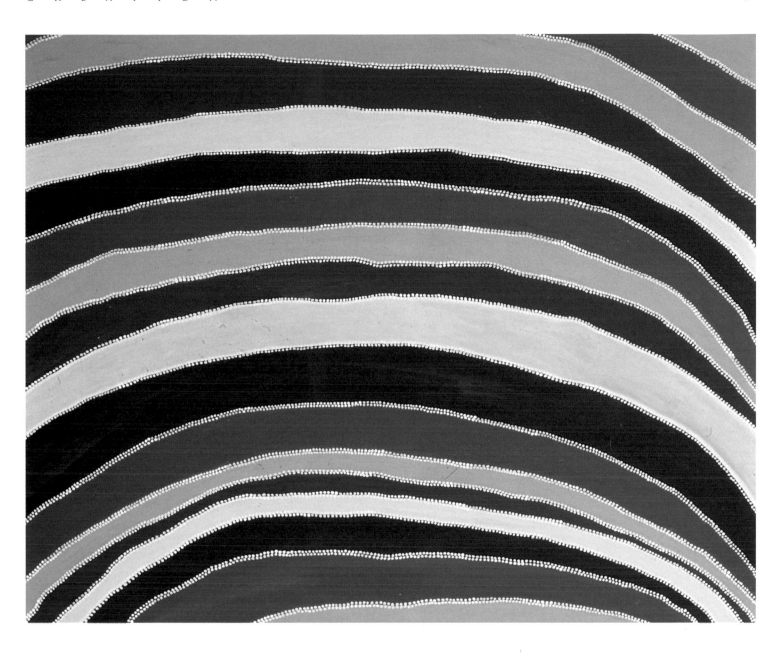

This painting by Freddie Timms, a Kija man living at Turkey Creek, Western Australia, represents Rainbow Dreaming which travels up from Yuendamu through the east Kimberley and centres at a site now beneath Lake Argyle. This site, now lost under water, is a sacred place and was once an ancient ribbon stone quarry. The multicoloured layers of stone reflect the beauty and power of the Rainbow Dreaming, and each band of coloured stone represents one of the tribes which inhabited this country from the Beginning. Courtesy Kimberley Art.

The frogs were very slow to come from below the earth's crust, for their bellies were heavy with water which they had stored in their sleep. The Rainbow Serpent tickled their stomachs, and when the frogs laughed, the water ran all over the earth to fill the tracks of the Rainbow Serpent's wanderings — and that is how the lakes and rivers were formed.[1]

Chapter Two

MYTHS OF THE ETERNAL DREAMTIME

When Creation myths are revealed through ritual and ceremony to honour the Spirit Ancestors, a sense of primal origins is evoked. For, as we have seen, the Spirit Ancestors, or Dreamtime Powers, simultaneously created Nature and culture, and laid the foundational pattern of living for human beings to follow.

THE RAINBOW SERPENT

This important Dreamtime myth relating to the beginnings of life, and to the central role played by the Rainbow Serpent in Creation, is described below by Oodgeroo Noonuccal. As has been mentioned, the Rainbow Serpent, although incorporating both male and female aspects, is generally considered female. In this account the Rainbow Serpent is the primary figure in the chronicle of Creation:

> In the Dreamtime all the earth lay sleeping. Nothing grew. Nothing moved. Everything was quiet and still. The animals, birds and reptiles lay sleeping under the earth's crust. Then one day the Rainbow Serpent awoke from her slumber and pushed her way through the earth's crust, moving the stones that lay in her way.
>
> When she emerged, she looked about her and then travelled over the land, going in all directions. She travelled far and wide, and when she grew tired she curled herself into a heap and slept. Upon the earth she left her winding tracks and the imprint of her sleeping body. When she had travelled all the earth, she returned to the place where she had first appeared and called to the frogs, 'Come out!'
>
> The frogs were very slow to come from below the earth's crust, for their bellies were heavy with water which they had stored in their sleep. The Rainbow Serpent tickled their stomachs, and when the frogs laughed, the water ran all over the earth to fill the tracks of the Rainbow Serpent's wanderings — and that is how the lakes and rivers were formed.
>
> Then the grass began to grow, and trees sprang up, and so life began on earth. All the animals, birds and reptiles awoke and followed the Rainbow Serpent, the Mother of Life,

across the land. They were happy on earth, and each lived and hunted for food with his own tribe. The kangaroo, wallaby and emu tribes lived on the plains, the reptile tribes lived among the rocks and stones, and the bird tribes flew through the air and lived in the trees.

The Rainbow Serpent made laws that all were asked to obey, but some grew quarrelsome and were troublemakers. The Rainbow Serpent scolded them, saying, 'Those who keep my laws I shall reward well, I shall give to them a human form. They and their children and their children's children shall roam this earth for ever. This shall be their land. Those who break my laws I shall punish. They shall be turned to stone, never to walk the earth again.'

So the law breakers were turned to stone, and became mountains and hills, to stand forever and watch over the tribes hunting for food at their feet. But those who kept her laws she turned into human form, and gave each of them his own totem of the animal, bird or reptile whence they came. So the tribes knew themselves by their own totems: the kangaroo, the emu, the carpet snake, and many, many more. And in order that none should starve, she ruled that no man should eat of his own totem, but only of other totems. In this way there was food for all.

So the tribes lived together in the land given to them by the Mother of Life, the Rainbow Serpent, and they knew that the land would always be theirs, and that no-one should ever take it from them.[2]

Another Creation myth relates to Ngalkunburriyayami, the female Rainbow Serpent from Arnhem Land. This myth focuses more on her daughter and son, and is described by Kunwinjku (or Gunwinggu) artist Thompson Nganjmirra:

Ngalkunburriyaymi is the daughter of Yingana, the first Rainbow Serpent of the Dreamtime, who gave birth to her and a son at the same time. The son, Ngalyod, became the most powerful of all three Rainbow Serpents and accompanied his mother over western Arnhem Land and the adjacent Croker and Goulburn Islands to create many sacred sites on land and on reefs. Ngalyod also became Controller of the Seasons: he can change their sequence if he becomes angry.

Ngalyod's sister prefers to confine herself to regions closer to her home near Nimbuwah rock where she gave birth to many children, an ability denied to her brother. Ngalkunburriyaymi, however, had the same power as Ngalyod to alter the shape of the terrain in order to create special places now declared as sacred sites. Aborigines living in the area know the caves, crevices, and waterholes where she usually rests, and they are careful to avoid any actions which might make her angry: the crying of children, the loud sizzling of food cooking on rocks, shouting, the trampling of vegetation, or approaching too close to any of her hiding places.

Those who anger Ngalkunburriyaymi run the risk of being swallowed. In the past, many Ancestral Beings transformed themselves into rocks, hills, waterholes, trees, plants, or other natural phenomena to escape her wrath. Those who chose to transform themselves rather than be captured by Ngalkunburriyaymi are known in their metamorphosed shapes as *djang,* objects in which their spirits live on forever. Such

djang are sacred sites; they are visited regularly by the Ancestors' descendants, who often perform ceremonies there. In this way Aboriginal people renew their spiritual links with the Ancestors, gaining renewed strength to cope with the daily problems of life.[3]

THE DJAN'KAWU

A major myth cycle from the north-east and central Arnhem Land recalls the journey of the wondrous Djan'kawu (or Djanggawul) Beings. The myth is older than the well-known Wauwalak Sisters (Wawilak or Wawilag) cycle which provides the basis for the *djunggawon*, *kunapipi* and *ngurlmag* rituals. The Wauwalak Sisters themselves are said to be really the daughters of the Djan'kawu, while the *kunapipi* and *ngurlmag* have both been introduced into Arnhem Land. The Djan'kawu myth provides the traditional basis for rituals known as the *Dua nara*. *Dua* is the name of the moiety (for a description of moieties see page 118) primarily concerned with this myth and its rituals. The other moiety, the *Jiritja*, is associated with a group of rituals known as the *jiritja nara*, linked to Laintjung, an Ancestral Being who is usually described in conjunction with his son Banaitja. 'The Djan'kawu, Laintjung, Banaitja and the Wauwalak are the principal Ancestral characters who, in eastern Arnhem Land, serve as institutors of religious ritual and ceremonial behaviour.'[4] The following myth comes from the region around Yirrkala in Arnhem Land:

Djan'kawu is the collective name for three Ancestral Beings — a male figure called Djan'kawu and his two sisters. The elder sister is called Bildjiwuraroiju or Bildjiwuraru, and the younger Miralaidj, Malalait, or Mandalaidj. The two sisters are associated with the sun and one of their totems is the red-breasted parakeet whose feathers are like the colours of sunlight.

In the Yirrkala mythic cycle the Djan'kawu leave Bralgu — the island of spirits — a place which they had originally come to from farther across the sea. In their boat they have brought with them several sacred objects that are still revered by the people of northern Arnhem Land today, including the *ngainmara* mat and the wooden *rangga* poles. In their travels across a stormy ocean they are guided by the rays of Bornumbirr — the Morning Star — and see many fish swimming around them. A whale rises up from the foam. Birds herald the dawn and the Djan'kawu arrive at Port Bradshaw harbour. After paddling past Garingan rock, they drag their canoe ashore at Jelangbara beach, they make wells by plunging a *mauwulan* walking stick into the ground and also 'plant' trees, which spring up when they stick their *djuda rangga*, or sacred poles, in the ground. Colourful birds nestle in the newly created trees and the Djan'kawu brother creates a sacred waterhole near the beach. Later he also installs goanna as part of the Dreaming by making it *wongar* (sacred).

The three Djan'kawu come to Wabinga Island where they meet the Baijini tribesfolk, who are considered by the Aboriginal people to be alien beings, and suggest that some of these people move to Dagu on the mainland. They leave ashes behind on the island and in this way the colour black becomes linked to the *Jiritja* moiety.

Later the Djan'kawu leave Port Bradshaw to search for a place where they can create a *nara* (ceremonial) shade. They travel on to Gagubam and to Caledon Bay where they establish sacred sites for the Kalu speakers. Then, looking up, they see large billowing clouds, called *wulma*, near Blue Mud Bay in both the Djapu and Djarlwak regions and leave many Dreamings here. All around the Port Bradshaw region, almost to Rose River, the Djan'kawu establish their cult, with the singing of songs and the ritual of the *Dua* moiety's *nara*, 'ritual', songs.

At Nganmaruwi, Bildjiwuraroiju becomes pregnant for the first time. In due course a baby boy is born then a baby girl. They are laid on a mat to protect them from the sun. Bildjiwuraroiju is careful not to open her legs too far for if she did, many more children would have come forth, for she stored them in her uterus (represented today by a conical shaped mat called the sacred *ngainmara*). Soon several children of both sexes are born. The Djan'kawu put the little boys in the grass so that later they would develop whiskers, but they hide the girls under the *ngainmara* mat to keep them smooth and soft, with no body hair. The Djan'kawu then departed. The children they created later grew up and married and became the progenitors of the Aboriginal people who live in this region today. From this time also the two sisters are continually pregnant.

Later in the myth, the Djan'kawu come to Mialbunjara (or Marabai) and the two sisters leave their sacred dilly bags in a shelter which they have made, and then go off to look for mangrove shells. The bags contain sacred *rangga* objects and emblems. While they are away, the Djan'kawu brother and several male offspring who have recently been born from the two sisters, sneak up, steal the dilly bags and make off with them. The two sisters hear the whistle of the *djummal* mangrove bird warning them that something is amiss so they run back to their shelter. They discover their sacred regalia missing, and tracks on the ground of the men who had stolen them. They follow the tracks to retrieve their sacred property but as they come closer to where the men are, the Djan'kawu brother begins to beat his *jugulung* singing sticks and the other men begin to sing. As soon as the women hear the songs they fall to the ground in fear and begin to crawl. They were too afraid to approach further, not so much of the men but because of the

Opposite: Elizabeth Djarrkman, of the Lamamiri-Wanguri clan from Elcho Island, Northern Territory, depicts two *Miyalk* (female Creation Ancestors) hunting for bush food. The Dingo Ancestor is shown as it is associated with this site. The animals at the top of the painting are also hunted for food. Courtesy of Coo-ee Aboriginal Art.

power of the sacred songs. In doing this, the men had stolen not only the songs of the women and their sacred *rangga*, but also the power to perform sacred ritual which, until then, was a power belonging only to the women. In this way did men assume authority over the sacred *dua nara* ritual — thereby taking power from the women which was rightfully theirs.

The sisters were initially in a quandary but later accepted that the men held their sacred *rangga* and allowed the men to look after the rituals. They agreed to spend more time collecting bush tucker at the same time realising that they really had lost nothing — they already knew everything so they could let the men have what was only a small part anyway. Apart from this, they held the knowledge that their uteruses were the real source of creative power and not just its symbolic representation as expressed in the rituals. Thus each sister retained her original creative power and potential with all of the associated sacred meanings.

Later in the myth the Djan'kawu brother introduces circumcision to the people of Nguruninana, near Elcho Island, although he does not actually circumcise himself.

Children continue to be born from both sisters as the Djan'kawu continue in their travels. At each place they visit, the children of the Djan'kawu sisters grow to adulthood and become the progenitors of the *Dua* moiety.

In the mythic cycle the conical mat or *ngainmara*, the symbol of the basket and the dilly bag, all seem to be connected to the uterus and are also linked with the creation of sacred wells across the landscape. The earth is fertilised through the waters of the sacred waterholes and Aboriginal people believe that spirit children come from these waterholes.

IMBEROMBERA AND WURAKA

Divine fertility and the creative power of the feminine principle also feature in the Dreamtime myth of Imberombera and Wuraka from the Kakadu tribes. In each place where she stops on her wanderings, Imberombera — who is the Great Mother — bears children and instructs them in language and culture. Meanwhile, her giant consort, Wuraka, although equally fertile, is exhausted by his potency and his only wish is to rest and join the sun in the east.

Wuraka came from the west, walking through the sea. His feet were on the bottom, but he was so tall that his head was well above the surface of the water. He landed at a place called Allukaladi, between what are now known as Mount Bidwell and Mount Roe, both of which he made. His first sleeping place, after coming out on to land, was at Woralia. He then came on to Umurunguk and so to Adkerakuk and Aruwurkwain, at each of which he slept one night.

The woman, Imberombera, also walked through the sea and landed at what is now known as Malay Bay, the native name being Wungaran. She met Wuraka at Arakwurkwain. Imberombera said to him, 'Where are you going?' He said, 'I am going straight through the bush to the rising sun.' The first language they spoke was Iwaidja, that is, the language of the people of Port Essington.

Imberombera had a huge stomach in which she carried many children, and on her head she wore a bamboo ring from which hung numbers of dilly bags full of yams. She also carried a very large stick or wairbi.

At a place called Marpur, close to where she and Wuraka met, she left boy and girl spirit children and told them to speak Iwaidja. She also planted many yams there and said to the children whom she left behind, 'Mungatidda jam' (these are good to eat).

She went on to Muruni, leaving yams and spirit children, and told them also to speak Iwaidja. From Muruni she went on, by way of Kumara, to Areidjut, close to Mamul, on what is now called Cooper's Creek, which runs into the sea to the north of the mouth of the East Alligator River. At Mamul she left children, one boy being called Kominuuru, and told them to speak the Umoriu language. The only food supply she left here was Murarowa, a cyprus bulb. She crossed the creek and went on to Yirrkala, but left no children there. This was close to the Kumboyu, Munguruburaira and Uramaijino, where she opened up her dilly bags and scattered yams. She went on to Jaiyuipali, where again she left food supplies. She searched around for a good camping place and, first of all, sat down in a water pool, but the leeches came in numbers and fastened themselves on her so she came out of the water and decided to camp on dry land, saying that she would go into the bush. Accordingly, she did so and camped at Imbinjairi. Here she threw the seeds of the bamboo, *koulu*, in all directions and also left children, one of whom was a boy named Kalangeit Nuama.

As she travelled along, Imberombera sent out various spirit children to different parts of the country, telling them to speak different languages. She sent them to ten places, in each case instructing them as follows:

Gnaruk ngeinyimma tjikaru, gnoro Koranger.
Watta ngeinuyimma tjikaru gnoro Kumboyu.
Kakadu ngeinyimma tjikaru, gnoro Munganillida.
Witji ngeinyimma tjikaru, gnoro Miorti.
Puneitja ngeinyimma tjikaru, gnoro Jaijipali.
Koarnbut ngeinyiia tjikaru, gnoro Kapalgo.
Ngornbur ngeinyimma tjikaru, gnoro Illari.
Umbugwalur ngeinyimma tjikaru, gnoro Owe.
Djowei ngeinyimma tjikaru, gnoro Nauillanja.
Geimbio ngeinyimma tjikaru, gnoro Waimbi.[5]

The first word in each of these lines is the name of a language which the children were to speak; *ngeinyimma* means 'you' or 'yours'; *tjikaru* is 'talk' or 'language'; *gnoro* is 'go', and the last word is the name of the place to which she sent them. Each of these places is regarded as the central camping ground of their respective tribes.

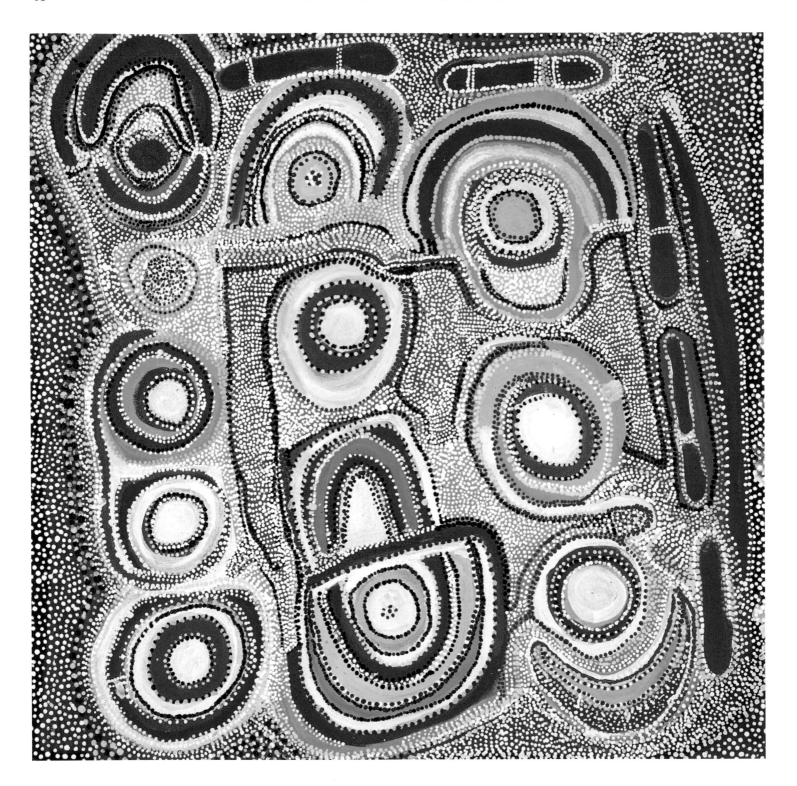

NAKARRA NAKARRA

A different kind of Creation myth is expressed in the following accounts of the important song cycle of the Nakarra Nakarra (Seven Sisters) Dreaming, which comes from the Wirrimanu (or Balgo Hills) community in the Tanami Desert near Halls Creek in Western Australia. The Nakarra Nakarra Dreaming track celebrates the journeys and actions of a group of women mainly from the Nakamarra kinship or 'skin' group in the Ngarangkarni (or Ngarranggarni) — the 'Dreamtime'. At times women from other skin groups appear in the narrative. The Nakarra Nakarra Dreaming track travels from south to north, from Parakurra (Point Moody) to the Yaka Yaka area, where it crosses the Wati Kutjarra (Two Men) Dreaming track. The doings of the Two Men, their Mother and other Ancestral Beings also feature in the song cycle. The aspect of the Nakarra Nakarra story that has received the greatest attention is the pursuit of the women by a man who is in 'wrong skin' or 'wrong way' relationship to them and must therefore be rejected. In the Wirrimanu version of the Dreaming, the women's suitor is a Tjakamarra, or classificatory brother. The full story of the women's travels covers far more than their pursuit by the Tjakamarra. It celebrates elements of the women's lives from food gathering and preparation to their participation in ceremony and their role in their sons' initiations.[6]

In Mirlkitjungu Millie Skeen's (a Kukatja Law woman) painting, reproduced here, she tells her story of the Nakarra Nakarra Dreaming:

> In the *Ngarangkarni* (the Dreamtime), seven Nakamarra (skin name) Sisters descended from the sky and travelled through the land. They were the first Women on Earth. They would come to Earth to hunt and gather bush tucker and to paint themselves and dance ceremony. The painting shows the women sitting down painting up before they danced at Parakurra and went on to Wangkaji. One day this old man, Tjakamarra (skin name), was walking past and saw them near the Nakarra Nakarra hills. He crept up on them and grabbed the youngest woman and took her away to be his wife, although he was son-in-law to the sisters. The other sisters ran away and ascended into the sky with their digging sticks. The younger sister fought back against Tjakamarra and got away. She followed her sisters up into the sky. The sisters are still up in the sky today. You can see the six sisters with the seventh sister following behind. [To a western viewer these are the Seven Sisters or the Pleiades stellar constellations.][7]

BIAMI AND MIRRABOOKA

The Creator figure Biami (or Baime) is one of the most important male Spirit Ancestors in south-eastern Australia. Much present-day mythology on Biami has been influenced by Christianity. Regarded by many as a Sky God, or All Father, and a central figure in Wiradjeri male initiation ceremonies, he was given his spirit form by the Rainbow Serpent during the Dreamtime. In the Beginning, Biami roamed the Earth living amongst the tribespeople and was always very busy guarding them. Now, while he is much loved as a protector of humanity, he watches tirelessly over Creation from his sky-home and punishes all who break the Law.

Oodgeroo Noonuccal relates a myth about Biami and Mirrabooka — the Southern Cross constellation:

> Biami the good spirit was kept very busy, guarding the tribes as they roamed throughout the earth, and he was very much troubled for them. He found that he could not watch over all of them at once; he knew he must have help to keep them from harm. Among the tribes there was a man called Mirrabooka, who was much loved for his wisdom, and the way in which he looked after the welfare of this people. Biami was well pleased with Mirrabooka, and when he grew old, promised him eternal life. Biami gave Mirrabooka lights for his hands and feet and stretched him across the sky, so that he could watch for

Opposite: *Nakarra Nakarra Dreaming* by Kukatja Law woman, Mirlkitjungu Millie Skeen. In this painting, Mirlkitjungu reveals aspects of the Nakarra Nakarra song line which relate how, in the *Ngarangkarni* (Dreaming), seven Nakamarra (skin name) sisters descended from the sky and travelled through the land. Finally, six of these women, with their digging sticks, ascended into the sky followed by the seventh sister who was pursued by a Tjakamarra (skin name) man. The seven sisters can still be seen in the sky today (the Pleiades) with the Tjakamarra — who became the Morning Star — trailing behind. Courtesy of Manungka Manungka Women's Association.

ever over the tribes he loved. And the tribes could look up to him from the earth and see the stars which were Mirrabooka's eyes gazing down on them.

When in later times white invaders came from across the sea and stole the tribal lands, they did not know that this group of stars across the southern sky was Mirrabooka, and they renamed them. They named Mirrabooka the Southern Cross. And the eyes of Mirrabooka they called the Pointers. But it is really Mirrabooka there, stretched across the sky; he will be there for ever, for Biami has made it so.[8]

KURIKITA AND WAKEND

Kurikita (or Gurigita), another important Ancestral Being, was the beautiful wife of Biami. She was completely covered with quartz crystals, so that when she turned, light would flash in every direction. She was lovely in form and always appeared particularly youthful and vital. In the Dreamtime, she left the Earth and went up into the sky to Wandanggangura — the place beyond the clouds. She is identified with the emu, called *jarawajewa* (the 'meat which is within'), who was her assistant totem. The emu-meat taboo is closely tied up with Kurikita, so she was a multi-dimensional Being. In addition, she is also the mother of Crow (Wakend, Waa or Wahn), a very important moiety Ancestral Being who is identified with night or shade and shadow. His moiety counterpart is Bunjil, the Eaglehawk. Crow is enjoyed as a trickster figure and is also connected to the star Canopus.

Myths about a conflict between two characters, Eaglehawk and Crow, have been recorded in widely separated parts of Australia. It is said that the most important focus of these stories has been the Darling-Murray river system in south-east Australia. The two moieties among the tribes of this area are named after Crow and Eaglehawk. The myths connect the moiety names with the tradition of conflict.

KARORA

The male creative principle plays an important role in myths which come from the Aranda (or Arrernte) tribe of the Great Western Desert. Karora, a male Ancestor Being, gives birth to animals and later to male children through his navel and armpits. Karora goes to sleep and dreams, and then awakes to find his new children. He inspires them with his *raiankintja*, 'call and dance', and then returns to a state of slumber beneath the Earth for all eternity. The following account comes from Professor Theodore Strehlow's *Aranda Traditions*. Strehlow was born at Hermannsburg in Central Australia and spent his youth among the Aranda.

In the very beginning everything was resting in perpetual darkness: night oppressed all the earth like an impenetrable thicket. The *gurra* ancestor — his name was Karora — was lying asleep in everlasting night, at the very bottom of the soak of Ilbalintja; as yet there was no water in it, but all was dry ground. Over him the soil was red with flowers and overgrown with many grasses; and a great *tnatantja* [ceremonial pole] was swaying above him.

This *tnatantja* had sprung from the midst of the bed of purple flowers which grew over the soak of Ilbalintja. At its root rested the head of Karora himself; from thence it mounted up toward the sky as though it would strike the very vault of the heavens. It was a living creature, covered with a smooth skin like the skin of a man. And Karora's head lay at the root of the great *tnatantja:* he had rested thus ever from the beginning.

As Karora was thinking, and wishes and desires flashed through his mind, bandicoots began to come out from his navel and from his armpits. They burst through the sod above, and sprang into life.

And now dawn was beginning to break. From all quarters men saw a new light appearing. The sun itself began to rise at Ilbalintja, and flooded everything with its light. Then the *gurra* ancestor was minded to rise, now that the sun was mounting higher. He burst through the crust that had covered him; and the gaping hole that he left behind became the Ilbalintja Soak, filled with the sweet dark juice of the honeysuckle buds. The *gurra* ancestor rose, feeling hungry, since magical powers had gone out from his body.

As yet he feels dazed; slowly his eyelids begin to flutter; then he opens them a little. He gropes about in his dazed state; he feels a moving mass of bandicoots all around him. He is now standing more firmly on his feet. He thinks, he desires. In his great hunger he seizes two young bandicoots; he cooks them some little distance away, close to the spot where the sun is standing, in the white-hot soil heated by the sun; the sun's fingers alone provide him with fire and hot ashes.

His hunger satisfied, his thoughts turn towards a helpmate. But now evening is approaching over the earth; the sun hides his face with a veil of hairstring, covers his body with hair-string pendants, vanishes from the sight of men. And Karora falls asleep, stretching his arms out on both sides.

While he is asleep something emerges from underneath his armpit in the shape of a bullroarer (a carved piece of wood that when twirled in ceremonies produces a roaring noise). It takes on human form, and grows in one night to a full-grown young man; this is his first-born son. At night Karora wakes up, because he feels that his arm is being oppressed with the weight of something heavy; he sees his first-born son lying at his side, his head resting on his father's shoulder.

Dawn breaks. Karora rises; he sounds the loud vibrating call known as *raiankintja.* The son is thereby stirred into life. He rises; he dances the ceremonial dance around the father who is sitting adorned with full ceremonial designs worked in blood and feather-down. The son totters and stumbles; he is still only half awake. The father puts his body and chest into a violent quiver — then the son places his hands upon him. The first ceremony has come to an end.

This rock painting, at Goose Camp on the South Alligator River in the Northern Territory, depicts Namarrkon (or Namargon) — the Lightning Man — and his wife Barkindj, the Binin (people) and the Devil Man, Namandjolk. Encapsulated in these forms is the interplay between lightning, rain and fertility in Nature's eternal cycle of renewal which is ritually celebrated by Aboriginal people in ceremony.

[In the myth Karora now sends his son to catch some more bandicoots for food. Meanwhile, over the next few days further sons are born to Karora during the night. One day the sons are out hunting once again for bandicoots and in the process they accidentally wound a creature with their *tjurunga* sticks that they thought was a sandhill wallaby. They hear the words of a song coming from the injured animal: 'I, Tjenterama, have now grown lame. I am a man as you are.' With these words the lame Tjenterama limps away.]

As they return to their father the sons are engulfed by the great *pmoara* flood, [brought by the Rainbow Serpent] of sweet honey from the honeysuckle buds coming from the east; it swirls them back into the Ilbalintja Soak. In all the present-day bandicoot ceremonies Tjenterama is represented as the great *gurra* chief of Ilbalintja. Karora, the natives say, remained behind at his original home: he is lying in eternal sleep at the bottom of the Ilbalintja Soak; and men and women who approach the soak to quench their thirst may do so only if they bear in their hands bunches of green *inuruna* boughs which they lay down on the edge of the soak. For then Karora is pleased with their coming and smiles in his sleep.[9]

NAMARRKON

In Arnhem Land — the 'Top End' of Australia — fierce lightning storms occur throughout the wet monsoon season. Images of Lightning Spirits can be found throughout this area in caves and on rock surfaces. As Aboriginal artist Wesley Nganjmirra, of the Kunwinjku people, has noted, some of these are sacred but can be viewed by outsiders, while others are both sacred and secret and cannot be seen by the uninitiated:

> The sacred site of Namarrkon, the Lightning Spirit for the Kunwinjku people living at Gunbalanya [Oenpelli], is about fifty-six kilometres [35 miles] away to the east of Nimbuwah rock, which towers into the sky from the surrounding plains. It is here that Namarrkon dwells throughout the dry season. Sometimes he assumes the form of a grasshopper to forage for food among the cabbage tree palms and bush shrubs growing nearby. He is also said to have created *aljurr*, ('Leichhardt's grasshopper') who goes looking for Namarrkon during electrical storms.

> When the wet monsoon season starts to build up in November, Namarrkon flies up into the sky and sits on storm clouds made by the Rainbow Serpent. From there he emits deep growls of thunder and sends lightning flashes across the sky, although no rain falls until the Rainbow Serpent releases it. This high vantage point allows Namarrkon to keep a close watch on Aboriginal people living below to see if they are observing codes of good behaviour, conducting sacred ceremonies, and passing on history and religion to the uninitiated in their tribe. If Namarrkon sees anything which displeases him, he plucks one of the stone axes from his knee or elbow joints and hurls it at the offender. Sometimes he misses and cleaves a tree in two.[10]

The lines running around Namarrkon's body and through his head and testicles represent the lightning circuits which give him great bodily strength and sexual prowess.

Various clan groups own different sacred sites related to Namarrkon. Lightning Dreaming sites are scattered throughout western Arnhem Land and adjacent islands. At some of these sites, paintings of Namarrkon may be found on the walls of caves or on exposed rock surfaces. As Arnhem Land painter Garry Djorlom has commented:

> All Kunwinjku clans acknowledge that Namarrkon is the powerful creator of lightning, and that his power is generated by the lines which surround his body and pass through his head and his testicles. . .

> Namarrkon does not select his victims at random: they have invariably committed some crime against Aboriginal Law and must be punished. Their bad deeds are clearly observed by Namarrkon from his vantage point high up in the sky, where he sits on a storm cloud. When he sees such a culprit, Namarrkon plucks a stone axe from one of his joints and flings it down in a brilliant flash of light. Usually he finds his mark with one strike, but if he misses, or if there are several people misbehaving simultaneously, he may use up more than one of his axes.[11]

SUN-WOMAN AND MOON-MAN

The eternal cycle of light and darkness may also be found in myths related to the sun and moon, and to the origins of day and night. Usually the sun is feminine, and the moon masculine. There are also implications here too, for the vital issues of life, death and rebirth.

A northern Australian myth tells how the Sun-woman, known as Wuriupranili, and the Moon-man, Japara, journey at different times across the sky. Each bears a torch of flaming bark, but when they arrive at the western horizon they extinguish the flames and use the smouldering ends to light their way as they return eastwards through the dark realms of the underground world. Each morning the fire which has been lit by the Sun-woman for her torch provides the first rays of dawn. The clouds of sunrise are reddened by the powdered ochre which she uses to decorate her body, and at this time the soft call of Tukumbini, the honeyeater, signals the beginning of a new day. Eventually Wuriupranili reaches the western horizon and once again daubs herself with red ochre, creating the beautiful and vivid colours of the sunset.[12]

Meanwhile, two Gunwinggu (or Kunwinjku) stories from western Arnhem Land also describe exploits of the Sun-woman and Moon-man. These myths have been used by the Aboriginal people as teaching stories for children:

> When the world was still new, the Sun-woman created a baby girl whose body shone with light. She lived in the west, beneath the ground, and continued to shine even as she grew older. When some other women tried to touch her, they burned their fingers as if in flames. When the women asked why this had happened, Sun-woman told them that both she and her daughter were 'Sun Dreaming. . .both of us'. Then she goes on to say: 'When all the land is dark, my daughter will bring you light. But I, myself, can't come up above the ground. I'm too strong. If I came up and looked at you all, up there, I would burn you to ashes.'
>
> The daughter continued to live beneath the earth with her mother and darkness fell across the land except on those occasions when the daughter would come up into the sky each day, lighting the country.
>
> Then she begins to think of her mother, lonely and waiting for her, and she goes down in the west on her way home. Down she goes, under the ground, to be with her mother, and darkness covers the land. They sleep there together until it is time for the birds to waken again. Then the Sun-woman sends her back to us. . .
>
> They made themselves Dreaming for us, so that we would have light every day to move about, and hunt for food. If we had no sun and there was night all the time, we couldn't find our way and we couldn't see any animals or plants. We would starve to death. The moon and the stars give us only a weak light, and the Sun-woman is too dangerous for us to see. But the Sun's daughter always looks after us; and every day she makes the country bright, to keep us alive.[13]

The second myth describes how, at the Beginning of the World two men came from the Goulburn Islands and the saltwater coast. One was Moon and other Djabu, the name of a small spotted bush cat.

In the myth the two men begin their travels, and survive by catching fish, collecting yams, hunting kangaroos and collecting goose eggs. Just after passing Red Lily Billabong they pull out their whiskers and plant them beside the water, where they transform into bamboo stems. For a number of days Moon and Djabu travel along the sand and finally make their camp high up on the rocks. They make a number of dilly bags, headbands and boomerangs, perform a ceremony, and in due course stay there for some time — trading the items they have made with neighbouring people. However, one day sickness comes upon the land and both Moon and Djabu feel that they may die. They put aromatic leaves upon the fire and try to steam themselves well again. They worry that if they were to die, no one would ever come alive again:

Djabu died first, but Moon was still alive because he was a clever man [traditional doctor or healer] and had plenty of power. He tried to revive Djabu, to make him come alive again, but couldn't. It was Djabu's own fault, because he didn't believe Moon and wouldn't help him to use his power to bring him back to life. He just lay there quite dead.

At last Moon grew tired of trying. 'All right,' he said. 'When I die, my body will come out alive again. I'll come up with a new body, because I'm a clever man.' But Djabu's body was dead for ever. Only his spirit stayed alive.

What Moon said was true. After he died, people looked up at the sky and saw him coming up again like new. All the men and women and children cried out, happy to see him. 'Ah!' they said. 'Here's that clever Moon! We saw him die, and now he has come back again!'

We could all have done the same as Moon. When we died, after three days our bodies could have come up new again. But Djabu made us go wrong, when he didn't trust Moon's power to bring him back to life. So now when we die, they just bury us. Our spirits stay alive, but our bodies can't come back. And it's all because of that Djabu.[14]

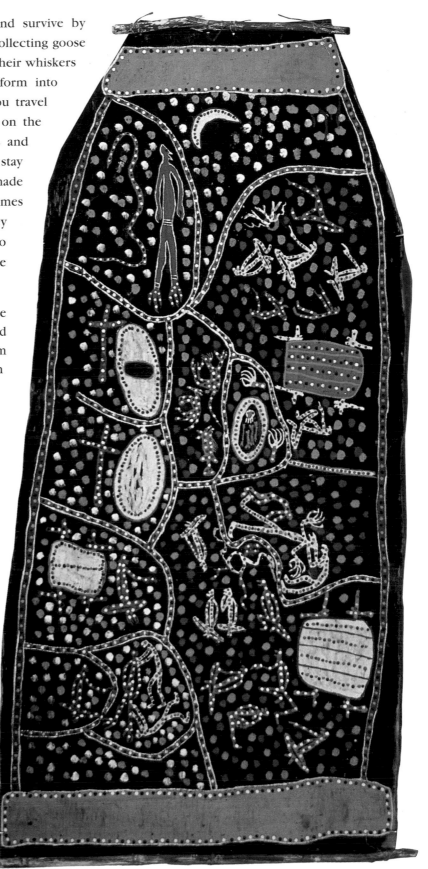

Waderi, Storm Wandjina
by Ngarinyin Law man,
David Mowaljarlai. Courtesy of
Coo-ee Aboriginal Art.

WANDJINA SPIRIT BEINGS

The north-west and central Kimberley region in Western Australia has striking rock shelter galleries and ancient cave sites which feature unique examples of particular Ancestral Beings — the Wandjina Spirit Ancestors — and also the Rainbow Serpent figures known here as Wunggud, Ungud or Galeru, with whom they are connected. Although Rainbow Serpent mythology occurs in many regions of Australia, the Wandjina are found only in the Kimberley, and are specifically linked to the Worrorra, Ngarinyin and Woonambal peoples who trace their descent from the Wandjina.

Wandjina figures seem eternal and unchanging because no changes or modifications to their form can be made by later generations of artists. In fact, the Aboriginal peoples of the region believe that all of the Wandjina figures represented in the rock paintings date from the *Lalai* or Dreamtime Epoch. It is important to remember that while in one sense the Dreamtime took place in the past, for all Aboriginal peoples it is also very much a sacred reality of the present, and that after the Wandjina Ancestors wandered upon the Earth, engaging in the various heroic deeds of the Creation, they later transformed into rock paintings. These paintings are considered sacred in the same way that the totemic Ancestors who metamorphosed into *tjurunga* (sacred object) stones are sacred throughout Aboriginal Australia. Today certain Aboriginal artists may reproduce Wandjina images on bark and other media, but only, as with all other Aboriginal people, if they have inherited the right to do this.

Unfortunately the Worrorra, Ngarinyin and Woonambal peoples have been displaced from their ancestral territories. This has shattered the intimate connection between these groups and the Wandjina Ancestors, and also means that the rock images are no longer being preserved by their custodial guardians in the ritual ways they were in the past. The names and symbolic meanings of these imposing mythic creatures have only been made available comparatively recently. As Sam Woolagoodja says in his poem, *Lalai Dreamtime:*

> Some *Wandjina* went under the land,
> they came to stay in the caves
> and there we can see them.
> Grown men listen to their *Wandjina.*

Long ago.
at another time,
these *Wandjina* changed the bad ones
into the rocks
and the springs
we always drink from.
These places hold our spirits,
these *Ungur* [eternal Dreaming] places of the *Wandjina*.[15]

Wandjina rock paintings tend to share various features in common. The heads are large and dominated by staring black eyes that at times resemble those of an owl — and interestingly, *dumbi*, the owl, is associated with the Wandjina figures in the Ngarinyin story of Wanalirri. As Mudrooroo has written:

It was in the *Lalai* — the Beginning, the Dreamtime — that the Wandjina appeared from the sky, with their heads surrounded by circles of lightning and thunder, and dressed in a curtain of rain. Thus they are connected with the sky, water and rain... Along with the cave images of the Wandjina are also images of the totems, or Dreamings, of that particular group of people. All Wandjina sites are *wunggud*, places of concentrated earth power and life-force, which is kept radiating by retouching the images or merely by visiting the sacred power site and singing the songs associated with it.[16]

The Wandjinas appear to have no mouths, and it is said that they closed their lips tightly when the first lightning bolt struck and have not opened them since. Some Worrorra people believe that the Rainbow Serpent sealed their lips, and it is also said that if the figures were to be repainted with mouths that it would then rain for ever. Daisy Utemorrah (1922–94), who was an elder of the Ngarinyin people taught that the Wandjina 'has no need of a mouth, he sends his thoughts'.

Other images are found in rock shelters — most commonly Rainbow Serpents and also Ngarra Ngarra and Wurula Wurula spirits of honey and bush fruits, *agula* (evil spirits) and representations of kangaroos, birds, fish, reptiles, plants and beehives.

The fertility of all species is believed to derive from the Wandjina. It is a responsibility of the custodians of the Wandjina Dreaming sites to ritually restore the images before the wet season so that these species would increase and the land would receive the nourishment brought by rain. This belief is further explained by Sam Woolagoodja in *Lalai Dreamtime:*

Those who have died are brought to the caves,
the bones are carried in to stay.
A man, like this, dies at last in his cave,
his spirit is free
to leave him and wait at its *Ungur* place...

At its own *Ungur* place
a spirit waits for birth.[17]

We love the earth and all things of the earth. Aboriginal

people come literally to love the soil,

and we sit or recline on the ground with a feeling of being

close to a mothering power...

In our view the earth is sacred.

It is a living entity in which other living things have origin

and destiny.[1]

Chapter Three

SACRED EARTH, SACRED LAND

To all Aboriginal peoples the land is sacred and is the well-spring of all life forms and the heartland of all being. In this sense, the Earth is perceived to be the Mother of all. In continuous seasonal cycles of birth, life, death and rebirth — all aspects of which have names, personalities and histories — this Mother feeds, clothes, shelters and nurtures all living beings. The land is '. . .blood of our blood, bone of our bone. . .', the Earth, to an indigenous person is inseparable from their own bodies.

Yami Lester, a Yankunytjatjara man from the north-west of South Australia, recalls learning about the land, people and culture as a child, when his parents:

> . . .just talked about the country. And I believed what they said. You couldn't doubt, it was just something real. The country wasn't just hills or creeks or trees. And I didn't feel like it was fairy tales they told me. It was real, our *kuuti,* the force that gives us life. Somebody created it, and whoever created it did it for us, so we could live and hunt and have a good time. That's how we come to be here because that *marlu* [the kangaroo] and *ngintaka* [the perentie lizard] created this image for us to live and breathe: the plants, the language, the people. And to have rain, wind and rain.[2]

In conjunction with the perceptions of the sacred Earth Mother as creator and nurturer of all species and the interconnectedness of all life forms, Aboriginal peoples have a particular relationship to their own beloved regional land, for it is here that the history of their Ancestral lineage is encoded and manifested. This is what is meant by the terms, 'country', 'my/our land'. This more intimate connection to a certain area of sacred land is determined by one's conception and birth sites, and one's inherited custodial land, for it is these that determine one's totem, moiety and entire web of social relationships and responsibilities.

So in traditional Aboriginal life it is not only the entire Earth that is held with reverence, it is also the specific country where one was 'dreamed' — that is, conceived from Ancestral Spirit, usually at a sacred water site where spirits reside awaiting rebirth. This home of their spirit is of fundamental importance to an Aboriginal person, for their 'home' or 'country' for the duration of their life is at the location of this conception spirit. Their spirit home is their home.

Opposite: Katatjuta (the Olgas) in the Northern Territory is an important sacred site to the Pitjantjatjara and the Yankuntjatjara peoples — or Anangu — and especially to the Aboriginal women of these tribes. Katatjuta has been translated as 'The Place of Many Heads' and several Ancestor Spirits are said to be associated with this site — most significant among these is Wanambi, the Rainbow Serpent. In this image two Ancestor Spirits, Ghee and Walpa, who are part of Wanambi, lie sleeping.

Also, this country exists in totemic and kin relationship to the territories of others — within the overall boundaries of Dreamtime patterning irrevocably established by the Spirit Ancestors. So the Dreamtime and the sacred land in one's custodial care are inexorably and intimately linked, and traditional Aboriginal women and men dedicate their lives to honouring Ancestral Law embodied in the land. It is not so much a question of 'my land' or 'my country' being owned by an Aboriginal person or group, but rather that *the land owns them*. The land and self is inseparable to an Aboriginal person, and thus is intrinsic to her or his identity. This concept is eloquently expressed by Galarrwuy Yunupingu, a Yolngu man from the Yirrkala community in north-east Arnhem Land:

> Land is very close to the Aboriginal heart and we can actually feel sorry for land, like you would feel sorry for someone who has been hurt. We give land ceremonial names as a sign of respect and this is very important, like respecting your elders. We acknowledge the land by giving it a title that is not used every day; a special name so we always remember what it means to us. When you address an Aboriginal elder you use an important sacred name to show their status as a person, and it is the same for the land when we name it.[3]

And as expressed elsewhere:

> The land is my backbone. . .I only stand straight, happy, proud and not ashamed about my colour because I still have land. I can paint, dance, create and sing as my ancestors did before me. I think of land as the history of my nation. It tells of how we came into being and what system we must live. My great ancestors who live in the times of history, planned everything that we practice now. The law of history says that we must not take land, fight over land, steal land, give land and so on. My land is mine only because I came in spirit from that land, and so did my ancestors of the same land . . .My land is my foundation. . .[4]

THE ABORIGINAL COSMOS

The concept of Earth or land in traditional Aboriginal cosmography is more extended than in European based cultures. It appears that in most, if not all, regional groups across Australia, a broadly similar world view developed in relation to the created world bequeathed by the Dreamtime Spirit Ancestors. The Earth was perceived as flat and circular, with the concave sphere of the sky reaching down to the horizon in all directions. But the sky was also a type of 'Earth' as well, and many Ancestral Beings and cultural heroes lived there. It was a land with a plentiful water supply and the stars in the night sky were the campfires of the Spirit Ancestors and heroes who dwelt in that realm. Beneath our own Earth, too, was an underworld populated by people and spirits much like ourselves. The afterlife is also believed to be a shadowy facsimile of this Earth plane. Whatever happens in this world also has resonances in the spirit World — there are no divisions. The entire landscape is viewed as one mighty arena in which the events of the Dreamtime Creation unfolded. Thus the cosmogonic Earth is seen as a sacred icon of great beauty, immense power and profound mystery inspiring great awe and respect.

SIGNPOSTS OF POWER

Integral to the journeys of the Ancestral Beings — the song lines, Dreaming tracks or song cycles — are the specific Dreaming sites of regional Aboriginal groups. The Dreamtime Spirit Ancestors in animal, human or some other form, moved across the countryside performing various tasks, creating, naming and also doing many of the everyday things that their Aboriginal descendants do to this day. In so doing they left markings, formations or indications of their spiritual presence in plant, animal and human form at particular places. Many of them 'made themselves' or 'turned themselves' into an aspect of the physical environment which infused that place with social meaning forever. To traditional Aboriginal peoples, as Catherine Berndt perceptively says:

> The whole land is full of signs: a land humanised so that it could be used and read by Aborigines who were/are intimately familiar with it, and read as clearly as if it were bristling with notice-boards. It is then the land which is really speaking — offering, to those who can understand its language, an explanative discourse about how it came to be as it is now, which beings were responsible for its becoming like that, and who is or should be responsible for it now.[5]

This echoes W. E. H. Stanner's observation: '. . .most of the choir and furniture of heaven and earth are regarded by the Aborigines as a vast sign-system'.[6]

As elder Maisie Cavanagh said at a recent Sydney conference: 'When one is walking through the land one must be quiet and respectful, walk carefully and listen. In this way the land may begin to speak to you.' And those who have walked through the Australian landscape 'in a sacred manner' with an Aboriginal person become aware of this truth. They walk through a personalised terrain full of signposts of direction and meaning, a sign language not apparent to an outsider. These signposted areas also must be deferred to and honoured. All Aboriginal people, who know the signposts and their meanings, tread with this deference and appear to know when and why others are behaving in like manner. Similarly, senior Aboriginal artists, carrying sophisticated symbolic maps of country in their mind's

Opposite: Artist Lily Karedada (Mindindil), a Woonambul woman, depicts a Wandjina, the rainmaker figure, found in caves throughout the Kimberley. Also shown in the painting is a long-necked turtle. Says the artist: 'If people go into a cave where the Wandjina stays, they must be careful not to disturb him. They must call out properly in the right language or a big cyclone might blow them away.' Courtesy of Coo-ee Aboriginal Art.

Overleaf: *Aboriginal Art and Habitation Cave* at Mount Borradaile in west Arnhem Land.

eye, seem able to recognise the abstract terrain and its meanings in the work of artists from other Aboriginal clans.

As we have indicated, to Aboriginal peoples the material world and the mythic or spiritual world are not two separate realms. There are various Aboriginal terms that approximate the English word 'spirit' but their meaning and applications are significantly different to western religious systems. As mentioned earlier, the term *djang* — used by the Gagudju tribe, for example, traditional custodians of the land now containing Kakadu National Park — describes the energy stored in a sacred Ancestral site.

The Pitjantjatjara people of the Western Desert use the term *kurunpa*, and believe that it is present in everything in the physical world. The Spirit Ancestors have bestowed their *kurunpa* upon the rocks, the trees, the plants, the animals — everything is alive and infused with spirit. Accordingly, Aboriginal people respect the spiritual forces which surround them and acknowledge certain customs and taboos as appropriate. A person approaching a waterhole, for example, may believe it prudent to throw a stone into the water to alert the Rainbow Serpent spirit of his or her approach, and in this way avoid the danger of being bitten.

The Ngarinyin people of the Kimberley region use the term *wunggud* to describe locations which possess sacred energetic power. According to Ngarinyin elder, David

Mowaljarlai, 'All Wandjina sites are *wunggud* —
places of concentrated Earth power. There is never
a cave, a painting site, without a *wunggud* water
(containing Earth energies)' nearby. A person will
always represent the totem of the *wunggud* site
where he or she was dreamt.[7] The totems were
bestowed by Wallanganda [Creator Being, senior
Wandjina], so that Aboriginal peoples would have
no reason to trespass on or fight for another's land
or food.

We can regard the land, then, as the central
cornerstone — or altarpiece — of Aboriginal
spirituality and a very direct and tangible link
between living human beings and the eternal,
mythic world of the Spirit Ancestors. The Dreamtime established the moral, social and spiritual
bond between all human beings, the Ancestral Beings and the natural world, and this has
resulted in a unity of being which all Aboriginal peoples respect and honour. As Eugene
Stockton has noted:

> The land is not just a surface over which the people walk, hunt and live out their lives.
> It is not the inanimate, unresponsive stage for the action play of separate individuals who
> are superior to it in being animate, sentient, intelligent, self-conscious, as the European
> instinctively views the land. Aborigines are confirmed by their religion with the
> conviction that the land, together with its people, flora and fauna, and everything else it
> contains, is a corporate organic whole, at least as animate, sentient, intelligent and self-
> conscious as any of its organic parts. The Aborigine feels part of this whole, enmeshed
> with the land in a real dynamic identity.[8]

BODY OF THE MOTHER

Many Aboriginal peoples regard the Earth as the Mother of all — as a sacred nurturing body
and the fountain of life. In essence, the entire sacred Earth, or the Great Mother, is one
extraordinarily abundant body. This body has all the usual organs and body parts, and has an
extraordinary history. Dealing with the fluctuating moods and disparate needs of her offspring
and relatives, she strives to maintain her physical and psychic balance amid the daily round of
activities and all that is constantly demanded of her by her very large family. She is endlessly
patient, tirelessly creative and has a continuously fertile womb to the degree that she is
compost fed, watered and nurtured with understanding, respect and tender, loving care.

The Ngarinyin people of the Kimberley region say that the whole of Australia is a distinct
human body lying on its back, belly up, in the ocean. Inside this body, which they call
Bandaiyan, is Wunggud, the Snake, who grows all of Nature on her skin. Bandaiyan is mapped,
or imprinted, by what the Ngarinyin call the *wunnun* system (the sharing and exchange
system and Law) which connects all Aboriginal people and which cannot be destroyed other
than by Australia being blown to pieces.[9]

Other Aboriginal peoples believe that the Earth and all its manifestations encompasses male and female aspects and is like a father, brother and sister — a beloved member of the family. Bill Neidje of the Buntji clan of the Gagadju shares some of his thoughts about his relationship to the land:

> Listen carefully this, you can hear me.
> I'm telling you because earth just like mother
> and father or brother of you.
> That tree same thing.
> Your body, my body. . .[10]

And Patrick Dodson, chairperson of the Council for Aboriginal Reconciliation, has stated:

> Land is a notion that is most difficult to categorise in English, but it is something that is very clear to me and to those people who belong to my group. Land provides for my physical needs and provides for my spiritual needs. It is a regeneration of stories.[11]

Another Aboriginal writer, Miriam-Rose Ungunmerr, of the Ngangikurungkurr people, has said that the 'countryside was somehow part of me and I was part of it. . .it was my home, it was me'.[12] Anne Pattel-Gray has similarly shared her personal reflections on the close bond that all Aborigines feel with the Earth:

> The Aboriginals are true lovers of Nature. We love the earth and all the things of the earth. Aboriginal people come literally to love the soil, and we sit or recline on the ground with a feeling of being close to a mothering power. . .It is good for the skin to touch the earth, to walk with bare feet on the sacred earth. . .The soil is soothing, strengthening, cleansing and healing. That is why Aboriginals sit on the earth instead of propping themselves up and away from its life-giving forces. For us to sit or lie on the ground is to be enabled to think more deeply and to feel more keenly; we can see more clearly into the mysteries of life and come close in kinship to other lives around us.[13]

Later she reflected further on these issues:

> We have always centred our lives in the natural-spiritual world. . . Only through our spiritual connection to the earth can we continue in our identity. This is why we conceive ourselves in terms of the land. In our view the earth is sacred. It is a living entity in which other living entities have origin and destiny. It is where our identity comes from, where our spirituality begins, where the Dreaming comes from; it is where our stewardship begins. We are bound to the earth in our spirit. By means of our involvement in the natural world we can ensure our well-being.[14]

For Aboriginal peoples, as we have seen, the Earth is the foundation of all life and is considered by many groups to be the Great Mother — with the surface regarded as her skin. To pierce her skin is to wound her. This holistic relationship between Aboriginal peoples and the Earth as Mother, and the related concept of the land as her skin, has been emphasised too by political events related to the mining of traditional Aboriginal lands — where savage and often irreversible changes of great magnitude are wrought upon the landscape with the economic justification of 'utilising primary resources'. The Woodward Royal Commission of 1974 made public to many white Australians for the first time the Aboriginal philosophy that it is not so

much a matter of land belonging to the people as of people belonging to the land, and that the relationship between Aboriginal peoples and the land is sometimes strikingly expressed by describing features of the land as parts of one's body. David Mowaljarlai, Ngarinwin Law man, has said:

> Disturbing sacred sites and land is agony for our people. Land and mountains and spring water — the heart of sacred sites — is really our body. Graders, bulldozers are pressing down on our body, liver, kidney bleeding. The spirit of the landowners is sickened. Graders are scraping the skin off our flesh — a sore that will not heal up: in my language, *wilu*, killing us.[15]

A number of elders are reported to have died as a result of the destruction of their sacred sites — which affected not only their vitality but also their ability to carry out their sacred custodial responsibilities.

David Mowaljarlai's comments are echoed in the words of Yolngu man, Mandawuy Yunupingu — Yothu Yindi bandleader and Australian of the Year in 1993 — describing the

Ochre pits in the
Northern Territory.

saddest day of his life when, as a young boy, he stood alongside his weeping father and watched in horror as a rock sacred to their beliefs was blasted apart: 'The mining company came with dynamite and bulldozers, the whole works. They just came and cleared everything and we couldn't stop them. . .'

One particular rock in that area of north-east Arnhem Land stood for the symbol of the dingo:

> It was significant to our beliefs but they just went ahead and destroyed it. It saddened my father's heart and he cried for it. I was saddened too when I saw my father crying. . .this was the land where I used to go together with my mother to collect yams, wild honey and fruit. Now it was all gone.[16]

Rich deposits of bauxite, aluminium ore, had been found in the thick red soil of the Gove Peninsula: 'They discovered the bauxite after the Second World War and they started to hassle us, saying they were going to come back and mine the land.'[17] In the 1960s, the Australian Government granted mining leases to a multinational company and excised most of the land from the Yirrkala Aboriginal Reserve, where Mandawuy and his family lived, without consulting the traditional owners.

Prior to her recent passing, renowned Ngarinyin elder Daisy Utemorrah also talked about the appalling devastation and insensitivity of multinational mining companies who have left 'holes' everywhere, where prior to this destruction, there were sacred sites of deep significance to her people. With a few mindless acts motivated by almost unimaginable greed, and within a handful of years, millennia of profound spiritual legacy is destroyed for all future generations.

For all Aboriginal peoples the whole visible and invisible environment is alive, and the entire Universe reflects principles of harmony, order and interrelatedness. The Earth Mother gives birth to all plant and animal species, even those that are potentially dangerous, like scorpions and death adders, are seen to have their place in the natural order. There may be exercises in control of certain species, but intrinsically all are seen to have a right to exist equivalent to that of human beings. There are no hierarchies in this system, only the natural attrition of life and the Spirit World; everything is part of the web of being.

In reflecting on the vitality of the entire Universe which pervades Aboriginal spirituality, and speaking in this instance of Koori people in New South Wales, Alex Grey, who worked on the Aboriginal Family Education Centres (AFEC) project between 1969 and 1973, commented in his final report on the communal, yet also individual, lifestyle which bonds Aboriginal peoples to the land:

> All life is one. They are of life, life is of them. To live their life harmoniously with all life is what life is all about. So they are of the land, and the land supports them if they are for the land, and what else it supports. They are conservationists and ecologists in terms

of their understanding of these concepts. This life is part of a stream of life that had its source in the Dreamtime, and continues on generation by generation through all life in the world into other lives in which sometimes they reappear in an organic form, though equally possibly in an inorganic form. This oneness, this globalness, this animism preoccupies. . .Aboriginal thinking to this day.[18]

It perhaps needs to be said, however, that 'animism' is an English word definition that attempts to describe the world view of indigenous peoples, but it does not convey the particulars of Aboriginal spiritual beliefs and relationships.

ELEMENTS OF THE EARTH

Many Aboriginal myths divide the land into different elements, each an Ancestral Spirit with its own history and personality. Earth is considered primary, and from it water must be liberated — this is the second element. From water, the third element, fire, must be released, and from it in turn — and symbolised by the smoke of a camp fire — air comes forth. Earth and water are considered to be female, and men must take special precautions when engaging with them, for the male Spirit Ancestors were born from them. Fire and air are incorporated in male initiatory rites — for example, in the *bora* circles (the sacred ritual spaces of Aboriginal ceremonial grounds). In male initiations the candidate must pass through fire and then be purified by smoking (a purificatory ritual carried out on other occasions). However, fire originally belonged to female Ancestors and symbolises their warmth and light. These Ancestors either gave or had their fire stolen by a male Ancestor such as Crow. He then keeps it for himself so somehow it has to be taken back from him. There are many stories about the original making of fire, and the stealing of fire, in Aboriginal mythology. In Arnhem Land, ancestral women were the possessors of fire until it was stolen from them by their sons, who became crocodiles. They in turn kept fire for themselves until it was retrieved by the rainbow bird who gave it to everyone.

The sacred colours of the Earth are red, black, yellow and white. These were given to the Aboriginal peoples during the Dreamtime, and also feature in the Aboriginal national flag (except for white). Red is the colour of blood, energy and fire, and represents the spiritual energy which connects all Aborigines with the Dreamtime and is found in potent locations within the Earth. It can also represent death. Black is symbolic of the Earth itself but is also associated with the marks left upon the land when the Spirit Ancestors made their campfires upon the Earth during the Dreamtime. Associations and applications vary in different regions but other examples are as follows: yellow represents liquids, and water in particular, as well as the markings upon the back of the ancestral Rainbow Serpent, and white is the sacred colour of the sky, the air and the stars. It is also the colour of the Spirit Ancestors who ascended to the heavens after their work was done on Earth during the Dreamtime.

Similarly underwater formations and the Earth's minerals are considered aspects left behind by Spirit Ancestors at particular locations, and as such have value which is spiritual rather than material. Among the most important of the minerals are ochre and quartz crystals. Ochre, or iron oxide, is the most important pigment used for body painting (and more latterly in 'art' making). Ochre comes in a range of colours, from white and yellow through to red and brown. In Aboriginal ritual life, red ochre, or *wiltja*, is the most sacred of all the colours. In parts of Central Australia it is associated with the blood shed by the dog Marindi, who died when he fought the gecko lizard Adno-artina. The blood of Marindi became the site of an important red ochre deposit situated at Parachilna in South Australia. The Adnyamathanha elders tell how, in the Flinders Ranges in South Australia, there lived a gecko lizard named Adno-artina:

> Every day Adno-artina would climb a high peak and challenge everyone to do battle. Marindi, the giant dog, heard his challenge. He bounded up the valley towards the gecko, barking his answer. Adno-artina looked at the giant dog, at his huge jaws and pointed teeth, and decided to play the trickster. 'I'll fight you later', he said. Marindi growled. 'Yes, you'll make a meal for my puppies.' He curled up at the base of the hill and went to sleep.
>
> Adno-artina waited until dark, then he issued his challenge again and, just to make sure that he would not lose his courage, he tied a magic string about his tail. Marindi leapt up and tried to seize Gecko by the back of his neck to shake the life from him but Gecko was too quick. He ran in beneath the dog's slavering jaws, seized the dog by the throat and hung on. Marindi tried to shake the lizard off, but could not. The sharp teeth ripped into his throat, red blood spouted out and formed the red ochre deposit found at Parachilna today.[19]

Marindi, the dog of this myth, appears to be one of the Melatji Law dogs whose Dreaming tracks start and stop over much of Australia.

Ochre colours may also be assigned to specific social groups and to particular ritual practices. In Arnhem Land red ochre is the sacred colour of the *Dua* (or *Duwa*) moiety and yellow ochre the sacred colour of the *Yiritja* (or *Jiritja*) moiety. Red ochre is associated with blood and death and is often used for sacred ceremonies. It is extremely important in desert cultures. Its great power derives from the belief that, as metamorphosed blood of the Spirit Ancestor, it cures, protects and strengthens. White ochre — sometimes called pipe clay — can represent peace, and also may be used for 'open' or less secret ceremonies. In ceremonies people 'paint up' their bodies according to the connections a colour may have in a particular myth associated with a sacred site in their region.

Choreographer for the Bangarra Dance Theatre, and Dance Co-ordinator for the Year 2000 Olympic Games, Stephen Page, says in relation to the dance composition 'Ochres', performed recently in Australia: 'The earth is part of the spiritual ceremonies of many clans, using ochres of different colours such as yellow, black, red and white. Ochre is applied in designs according to your totem, so that your totem spirituality is awakened during the paint up. There are no time constraints, no boundaries, there's an apparent timelessness around the ritual.'[20]

Ochre is also used in mortuary rituals in some areas. For example, one of the oldest skeletons found at Lake Mungo, now known as Mungo Man, had been anointed with ochre, which also surrounded the body. The skeletal remains of Mungo Man have been dated at an astonishing 36,000 years ago — an unequivocal example of the existence of Aboriginal metaphysics and complex burial practices long before conventional speculations had estimated. Ochre is frequently found at archeological sites, and in some cases has also been utilised in attempts to determine dates of rock art paintings.

Quartz crystal is said to be possessed of magic properties and when a 'clever' man or

woman (traditional 'doctor' or healer, shaman, magician, witch, witchdoctor, diviner or curer in English) is 'made', they receive an empowered piece of crystal which they keep hidden and away from the eyes of the uninitiated. It can be used in healing and in harmful practices. To effect a cure, the clever man rubs or presses the crystal over the affected part, while chanting a spell. He then sucks the part and extracts a foreign body which is the cause of the trouble. This may be a slither of bone, stone or wood.[21] Marnbi, the bronze-winged pigeon, is associated with gold (his blood) and white quartz crystal (his feathers). The Adnyamathanha elders narrate the myth which connects him to these minerals:

> Once a man made a net to catch bronze-winged pigeons. A flock of them came along and he flung the net over them. He struck at them with his club, but one of them, Marnbi, somehow managed to escape. He rose into the air and fled, dropping feathers and specks of blood as he went. At places where he rested, he left more blood and feathers, and these became a source of gold and quartz. He flew into New South Wales and went north to Mount Isa where the big mine is still operating. He also threw a firestick high into the air and when it hit the ground sparks flew off in all directions which became opals. This site is near Coober Pedy, a large opal mining area.[22]

Embedded within Aboriginal Dreamtime mythology is knowledge of ancient planetary and geological history. To give an indication of the extent of this ancient and accumulated knowledge, renowned Aboriginal story-teller Alinta — also known as Lorraine Mafi-Williams — teaches that whenever her Aboriginal elders talk about the Beginning — the Dreamtime Creation — and their history, they always talk about the time when the Earth was one land mass. This one Earth land mass — known as Gondwana or Gondwanaland — existed prior to

Uluru (Ayers Rock). A very important sacred site of the Pitjantjatjara and the Yankuntjatjara peoples — the Anangu — lies in the very centre of the Australian continent. A place of pilgrimage for Aboriginal peoples, Uluru was the site of a battle which marked the end of the *Tjukurrpa* (the Dreamtime) Creation era.

the cataclysmic Great Floods, which resulted in the World being split into different continents with certain areas of the land being sunk below sea level.

Similarly, in Kimberley lore the Napier Range was understood to be a Great Barrier Reef in the ancient Gondwanaland Sea.[23]

The break-up of Gondwana happened in the late Palaeozoic times and, in the Pre-estuarine period, which commenced during the height of the last Ice Age around 18,000 years ago, the sea was 150 metres (164 yd) lower than at present and a land bridge connected Australia to Papua New Guinea and continental shelves extended to the vicinity of the Indonesian Islands. Aboriginal peoples, on current archeological estimates, are believed to have continuously lived on this continent for around 100,000 years — and perhaps even longer...

Knowledge of these ancient events, incorporated into the Dreamtime mythology, was transmitted orally — in ceremonial song, dance, painted boards, *rangga* and *tjurunga* (sacred objects) — through countless generations, and it is only in the, comparatively brief, last 200 years that this living mythology has become fragmented due to ignorance and the brutal practices of the invading English colonists, pastoralists and more recently, as we have said, politically sanctioned multinational corporations and the passing of elders who were raised in the traditional ways.

SACRED SITES

We have already noted that for all tribal Aborigines, the most potent sites of power are those sacred locations where Spirit Ancestors either burst through into the landscape during the Dreamtime, or withdrew from it to a state of eternal vigilance. These sites are the places with *djang*, *malagi* or *wunggud* — and other names, depending on the language group. As Bill Neidjie says of *djang*: 'That secret place...Dreaming there...Because that *djang* we sitting on under, e watching that *djang*, what you want to do. If you touch it you might get heavy cyclone, heavy rain, flood, or e might kill some other place... other country... e might kill im.'[24]

These sacred sites are 'strong' because they have been sanctified energetically by the Spirit Ancestors. As well as providing Earth energy to all living species, they are also the locations of spirit children, and the importance of these sites is symbolically reaffirmed by ceremonial and ritual activities at these sacred places.

Perhaps the most famous of Australia's sacred sites, and a place of pilgrimage for peoples of all nationalities and creeds, is that huge red monolith known as Uluru (or Ayers Rock) situated in the very centre or navel of the country. According to Mudrooroo, Uluru is a telluric or *djang* place of amazing potency and it is 'perhaps the most sacred place for Aboriginal peoples right across the country, for here the many song lines and Dreaming tracks come together in a unity of myth which is celebrated by the giant sandstone monolith', which rises nearly 400 metres (1312 ft) above the surrounding plains. The monolith was apparently built

...in the *Tjukurrpa* or Dreamtime by two boys who played in the mud after rain. When

Artist Beerabee Mungnari, a Kija man, says of his painting: 'This is Purnululu (the Bungle Bungles) country. Dreamtime Wound from fighting long ago with spear, *boomerang* and *ngula ngula*.' Courtesy of Coo-ee Aboriginal Art.

Katatjuta (the Olgas), sacred site in the heart of the Northern Territory, bathed in the pink-red glow of imminent sunset.

they had finished they travelled south to Wipunta, on the northern side of the Musgrave Range, where they killed and cooked a euro, then turned north again and made their way to table-topped Mount Connor, where their bodies are seen today as boulders. In the Dreamtime Uluru was the scene of epic battles which marked the end of the Dreamtime Creation period — the scars of which are etched in the rock. The custodianship of Uluru is with the Pitjantjatjara and Yankuntjatjara peoples and ownership has been inherited from both mothers' and fathers' sides. The rock itself is divided into the sunny side and the shady side, which not only refers to generational

divisions but also to the division between two great myth cycles whose central themes motivate most of central Australian Aboriginal society.[25]

Another magnificent and very powerful *djang* site is Katatjuta (or the Olgas). Katatjuta is a very sacred place whose specific ritual associations can only be mentioned by initiated Aboriginal elders. It is approximately 50 kilometres (31 miles) west of Uluru and is made up of more than 50 domes of rock rising about 600 metres (1968 ft) above the otherwise flat surrounding countryside. It is estimated that Katatjuta was formed about 600 million years ago.

Katatjuta has been translated as 'The Place of Many Heads' and a number of Ancestral Dreaming Spirits are said to be associated with this site. Chief among these, and symbolised by the largest monolith, is the Rainbow Serpent Wanambi, who lives in one of the waterholes on top of the tor during the wet season. However, during the dry season Wanambi makes her way to one of the gorges and enters the rock. So part of the site is sacred to the Rainbow Serpent and it is forbidden to light fires in the area or drink at the waterhole, lest Wanambi become angry and rise to attack. Many parts of Katatjuta refer to Ancestral Women — for example, the caves on the southern side of the 490 metre (1607 ft) high Walpa Gorge. It has also been reported that these caves were once piles of corkwood tree blossoms collected by the Corkwood Sisters of the *Tjukurrpa* or Dreamtime. On the eastern side are the camps of the Mice Women and the Curlew Man, whose myth formed the basis of a fertility ceremony (curlews are guardian birds and carriers of the departed souls to the Sky World). One highly spectacular pillar of rock at Katatjutu is the transformed body of Malu the Kangaroo Man dying in the arms of his sister Mulumura, a Lizard Woman. Malu was killed at this place by a pack of dogs after his long journeying from the west. His mortal wound is an erosion in the rock and his spilled intestines appear as a rock mound at the base of the pillar. Other stories relate the tale of the Pungalunga Men and the Ancestral deity, Yuendum, who gave humankind plant foods.[26]

Aboriginal peoples have always needed to make pilgrimages to their sacred places to conduct ceremonies. These spiritual journeys have been called 'walkabout' in English and often with a pejorative undertone to indicate a certain 'aimless' wandering by Aboriginal peoples. Nothing could be further from the truth. Aboriginal people have never been aimless wanderers, neither are they nomadic in the literal sense. Their pilgrimages often entailed arduous walks for hundreds of kilometres and, rather than being 'aimless', they have always followed well delineated paths across the land. These paths are the original Dreaming tracks or song lines mapped by their Ancestor Spirits, which Aboriginal peoples have re-enacted, when possible, for tens of thousands of years. Pilgrimage or 'walkabout' mirrors the eternal movements of the sun, moon and stars. Stellar positions also influenced the direction of pilgrimages, as they did other aspects of Aboriginal life.

It is clear that all Wandjina sites are *wunggud*, places of concentrated Earth power:

> In my youngfella time, the older people used to teach us: 'Whatever law Wandjina gave, we have to look after all these things. Don't muck around with them or that Wunggud will get shock, because you are damaging Wallanganda's [Creator Being, senior Wandjina appointed by Ngadjar — the Above One, Master of All Galaxies] creation. You are misusing his gift to us from Creation Time. It is mahmah [sacred],' they told us.[27]

Many of the ceremonies, rituals and songs that are central to Aboriginal culture are 'owned' by those who have been initiated into the religious cults associated with the mythic cycles of specific Spirit Ancestors, who are in turn linked to particular sacred sites. With age, the younger initiates gain more and more knowledge about these Ancestral Beings from the elders of the tribe. As we have seen, these sites have *djang, wunggud,* or sacred energetic power, and it is distressing for Aboriginal people to have to prove their ownership of land, for example in land claim disputes, by having to reveal secret or sacred information to uninitiated people. Custodians of this knowledge also feel an obligation to protect uninitiated people from the power that is stored at these sacred sites.

Among different regional groups, this sacred knowledge of myth, song, ritual and ceremony

Warnngayirriny (Jack Britten), a Kija man, shows the country in the Kija estate known as Jarlarloon — the place of the shitwood. It is characterised by *Goowarle-warleny* (small round hills) and shitwood trees. It also includes the *Booraj* (ceremonial designs) for Jarlangarnany (the 'plains' kangaroo) which lives in the Jarlarloon country and which were painted on young men when they were initiated. Courtesy of Kimberley Art.

— linked with sacred sites — is passed orally from generation to generation. This knowledge also relates to the meaning of 'country', and has a practical function — it helps to differentiate groups of people from each other and also defines tribal rights to land and resources. Such knowledge is never the sole possession of an individual but is held by a group of people who have been initiated into custodianship of that land and therefore have a right to the sacred information that is associated with it. Traditionally, this information is not to be revealed to the uninitiated.

There is also a deep respect between neighbouring Aboriginal groups whose countries share common boundaries. When an Aboriginal person approaches a sacred site, she or he does not approach by the most direct route but by the same route as taken by the Spirit Ancestor associated with it. Such Dreaming tracks may pass through the 'countries' or territories of local clans and tribes. As a result, all Aboriginal people, irrespective of tribal affiliation, who share a Dreaming track of a Spirit Ancestor or Ancestors, 'have a secret bond of friendship and a mutual claim to hospitality and protection. This enables members of a cult group which is responsible for the myths and rites associated with the hero of the path, to travel safely along that hero's path even when it leads into other tribal territories. . .[28]

Through the mythology of the land, various local groups and tribes have thus become mutually dependent on each other for their religious life. As discussed earlier, each group is a custodian of a chapter of a particular myth and of the specific sacred sites and religious rites associated with it. However, full assurance for the present and future can only be maintained and gained by a knowledge of the myth as a whole and the performance of all the rites.

Matingali (Mati) Bridget Matjital, a Ngarti Law woman, in this Dreaming painting of her country, shows Ngarti women out in the desert hunting for food. They all have their *luwantjas* (wooden dishes) to carry the food they find back to camp. Many different foods are available, including *lukararra* (grass seeds), *yakatjirri* (mistletoe berries) and the fruit from the *wiltjilki* tree. Courtesy of Coo-ee Aboriginal Art.

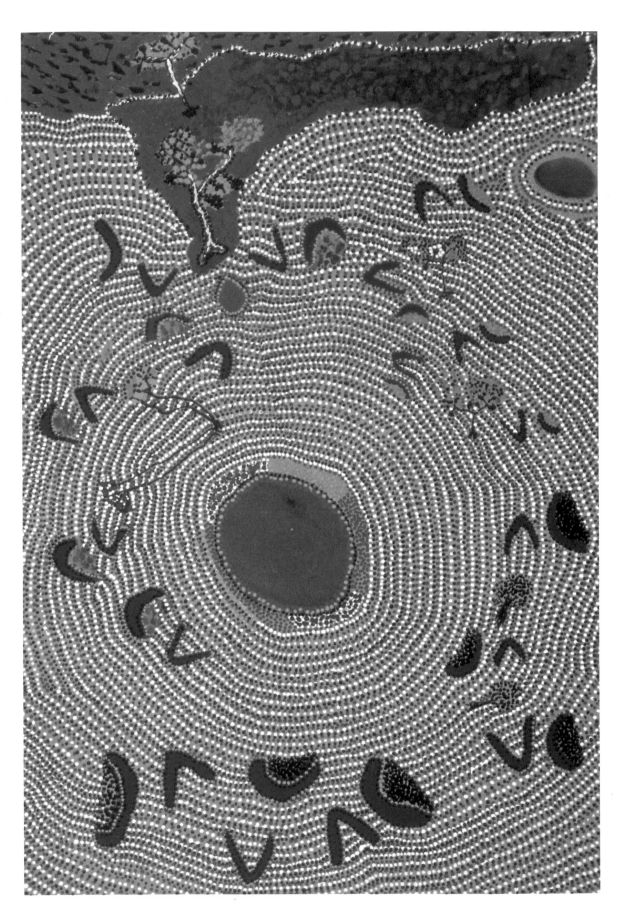

Senior Law woman, Matingali Bridget Matjital Napanangka, of the Ngarti people, from the Wirrimanu community in the Tanami Desert in Western Australia, in excerpts from a conversation with author Anna Voigt, gives glimpses into the affectionate relationships and responsibilities between country and family, and also into the seamless web that is the eternal Dreamtime and present time:

Anna Voigt: You look after country?

Martingali Bridget Matjital (Mati) Napanangka: From my mother. . .From mother. Grandfather. Uncle. From auntie. . .My mother tell 'im about me: You look after 'im country. Don't forget for country. Still we make 'im I still stopping la Yaka Yaka from my country. From mother country. From my grandmother. [Mati's mother says, Don't forget your country. Don't forget those songs.]. . .Yeah. Nakarra Nakarra [Dreaming song line]. Still Tjipari [another Dreaming track]. One now. . .We bin dance 'im before. My mother and granny, grandmother.

AV: And did your grandmother take you hunting and show you your country?

MM: Yeah, all around [different places]. You know, I bin take 'im you. We bin little girl that way. . .Yeah. And we been at Sturt Creek [on a cattle station where Mati worked as a domestic]. We never bin forget for Ngantalarra, for Nakarra Nakarra, for Yaka Yaka, nothing. [While at Sturt Creek Station, Mati was still able to leave and go to Ngantalarra and dance the Nakarra Nakarra.]

AV: Travelling through the country?

MM: Yeah, Yeah. *Palya* [good]. I not forget for that culture, you know? Still we bin work around. Granny bin take 'im about me. Granny bin say la me, I know. I can't forget for that ceremony. We got that Law. We gotta hold 'im, we can't lose 'im. Hold 'im tight.

AV: So, she teach you not to forget?

MM: Yeah. We can't lose 'im. Hold 'im tight. . .[Pause]. . .Yeah. Camp. Walk around. Take me from mother. Take it away from big fire and sleep. Mother and daughter.

AV: Mother and daughter.

MM: [Laughs] Grandmother.

AV: Your grandmother, mother and you go together in the country? And she'd show you?

MM: Yeah. Show me soakwater, and river, and creek, you know. What for all bin do 'im Dreaming Time, and telling me story from Dreaming Time. Where bin hunting, tell me. Huntin round. Get 'im *tjirrilpatja* [bush carrots]. Yeah, and bush onion and *mulupuka* that tree . . . That tree where I bin singing *corroboree.*

AV: And that's where a lot of them walked, following the snake's trail?

MM: Bush tucker there when we go. . .*Coolamon.* Bush fruit, *tjunta* [bush onion], *kumpupatja* [bush tomato], *tjirrilpatja* [bush carrot]. Hunting, seedpa [seeds] *ininti* seed. . .Everywhere. Seed, *ininti* seed. [Starts singing, beating time to herself.] You got 'im painting [Wallupanta]. You can have 'im painting. From my mother. . .Ah, you gotta talk, you.

AV: Me?

MM: Yeah. From Napanangka, yeah. Mother for you. From mother, Napanangka [Mati]. From Nakarra Nakarra you can think. Him [her, you] daughter for Mati. Daughter for me.

AV: Me?

MM: Yeah, Nakarra, Uwai [yes]. Yeah.

Matingali's family activity is also in the song cycle. The going out into country, the hunting and the gathering — as it was in the Dreamtime so it is today. So everyday activities come into the song cycles with the mythological references — it is a combination of singing, dancing, hunting, gathering food and other activities — all existing in relationship with each other and all events having accompanying emotions and feelings. Though the food hunted and foraged is not simply food, it has been created by the Ancestors in a mythological sequence.[29]

. . . Each vein of mortal man and mountain rock

of animate totem and primal path, lodes layering

a vast inter-connected polyglot pattern

that was his life —

Borne into spirit, danced

to his father before him and sung

to his grandfather before that . . . [1]

Chapter Four

SONG LINE, MUSIC AND DANCE

From an Aboriginal perspective the Australian continent is literally enmeshed and crisscrossed with a variety of sacred sites and their accompanying mythic songs, stories and meanings. This mnemonic song line mapping constitutes the creative journeys of the Spirit Ancestors and the markings of specific locations where the Spirit Ancestors first arose from the Earth, ascended to the sky, came ashore from across the seas, engaged in intensely creative acts and where they later departed to seek their rest at the conclusion of their divine Creation. These sites, as we have mentioned, are known as 'strong energy source' places — or *djang*, *wunggud* or *malagi* places, according to regional languages. They are believed to contain powerful spiritual energy or spirit essence, bestowed and sanctified by the Spirit Ancestors, which can be drawn upon and recharged through ritual activity. The sites are like electrical sockets or high energy points in a grid system, and can be joined up like dotted drawings showing the song lines of the Ancestors.

The mapping of sacred sites and song lines was also one of encoding Divine Law. These regional areas are connected to other regional areas, some of which may contain continuing aspects of a Dreaming track or paths of Ancestral journeying, so there are mutual obligations inherent in this knowledge. An Ancestral song line, or song cycle, may traverse thousands of kilometres across several language areas.

Each song in a cycle, which signifies an action of an Ancestral Being in a specific place, is owned and is the responsibility of an Aboriginal person who is the custodian of the Dreaming of that place. Each custodian has been taught the procedures of her or his duty of care to the land, and they expect that all other Aboriginal custodians of a Dreaming track would similarly carry out their roles — for a Dreaming track, or song line, connects all those who share in this Dreaming and the knowledge it contains. The whole cycle had to be completed by each in turn at the specified site — the omission of one song of a cycle would literally 'make a hole' in the song line. With this interdependence and execution of individual and collective responsibility, the health of peoples and land was maintained — for they were seen as inseparable.

All of these patterns for living were laid down by the Spirit Ancestors and are irrevocable Law to an Aboriginal person. To transgress the Law has dire consequences, and Aboriginal

Men's *corroboree* performed at Yuelamu community, Mount Allen, Northern Territory.

peoples are aware that the Ancestors are always present and watching. Needless to say, the disruption and fragmentation occasioned by brutal European invaders, heedless of Aboriginal rights, spiritual canons and responsibilities, has had devastating consequences to the holistic continuity of this Aboriginal Law, bound as it is in sacred relationship with a sacramental land.

Aboriginal music is probably the only truly Australian music. Unlike the music which has been composed since white settlement of this country — which by its very nature is eclectic and invariably draws on a wide range of international influences, both classical and contemporary — Aboriginal music has been here for as long as Aboriginal peoples have lived on this continent, and is intimately connected with the land. Aboriginal songs are creative expressions of the profound spiritual traditions of the eternal Dreamtime. Indeed, the land was sung into Being as the first songs were sung by the Spirit Ancestors themselves, and these songs have passed down through countless generations of custodians to the present day. Each song is a celebration of the unique role of a Spirit Ancestor within the sacred landscape — each song an integral part of Creation itself — for these songs delineated the paths that had been taken by the Creator Beings as they journeyed across vast sections of the terrain: the songs actually sanctified the sacred sites that had been created along the way. It was as if the land were enmeshed in sacred music through these

song lines — a rich mythic tapestry woven by the Ancestors as they wrought their creative magic upon the Earth. For thousands of years individual custodians, or 'owners', of the land have guarded these sacred song line territories and the myths and ceremonial practices associated with them. Through the song lines each area of the land was linked from region to region, each song a vital contribution to the whole.

The Ancestral song lines also gave important geographical information providing the locations of food and instructions on how to hunt, forage and prepare these foods. Though food is not simply food — it is also ancestral spirit. And, most importantly, the Ancestors generally followed water routes — across country from waterhole to waterhole or alongside rivers — and thus related sources of life-sustaining water. They had many encounters and adventures,

Above: Johnny Mosquito Tjapangarti, a Kukatja man, constructing a sand painting. Courtesy Coo-ee Aboriginal Art. Opposite: *Burradoo* (Meeting Area) by aclaimed artist Rover Thomas (Joolama), a Kukatja-Wangakajunga man, who says: 'Burradoo is a rain place where everyone meets to dance *Wonga*. Blackfellas from Bedford Downs, Halls Creek, whatever, all meet here.' Courtesy Kimberley Art.

The kookaburra of the kingfisher family is considered a protector by Aboriginal people and is distinguished by its gurgling, laughter-like call. Bird call is 'talking' rather than 'singing' in Aboriginal cultures — only humans can sing.

created people and other creatures, moulded natural features, gave language and named all that they did. They performed ritual and ceremony along the way to mark both places and events in their travels thus instituting rites and practices for their descendants to follow. The song lines are at one and the same time metaphysical, physical and social maps. All Aboriginal Law is encoded in the Ancestral song lines or song maps, and thus they are the anchors and signposts for the culture.

As the Ancestors bestowed their grace through song, Aboriginal music has always been primarily vocal. For the most part these are the songs and ceremonial chants of the Dreaming tracks which have had only minimal musical instrumentation as an accompaniment. All across the country Aboriginal people created their rhythms by clapping their hands, slapping their thighs and knocking clapsticks (or song sticks) or boomerangs together. On some ceremonial occasions women clapped their hands or beat a clapped hand against their thighs, while at other times they might create an accompaniment by beating their hands or sticks on rolled possum skin rugs. Sometimes *didjeridus* were also used. Played only by men and found predominantly in the northern part of the country, these long tubular instruments were fashioned from hollow branches of a tree. When the musicians blow through them by pursing their lips and using a special circular breathing technique, deep and sonorous tones come forth. Overall, Aboriginal musical rhythms were created as a fusion of ground and body thumping, percussive high-pitched clapsticks, and the deep bass dronings of the *didjeridu*.

In some ceremonies there would be periods of singing and also times when the words within a song might be spoken, the spoken sections usually relating to bird or animal sounds. The sounds of Nature, such as birds, are perceived as 'talking' for only humans can 'sing'. The most sacred sections of a ceremony would be those describing secret aspects of a Creation story, and the words sung at this time would be those believed to have come directly from the Spirit Ancestors themselves. In ceremonies which were not completely closed, or reserved for initiates, sacred information of this sort would be cryptically encoded and thus not fully revealed. It is important to remember that the words of a ceremonial song are not simply 'words' in a literal sense — they are utterances that relate to the very fabric of Creation. Even the more recent 'little history' songs are not 'composed' or 'written' like lyrics, but are dreamed into existence. They come straight from the Spirit Ancestors, and are imbued with sacred vitality and strength for this reason.

While at various times Aboriginal music would certainly have served as an entertainment — as an exuberant expression of everyday life — there can be no doubt that its primary role is one of spiritual celebration. As musicologist Catherine Ellis has written: 'The songs. . .convey all the emotional and spiritual associations with a particular being in a particular locality.'[2] Ceremonial participants had to learn and remember each song very accurately because each detail of the musical performance related to different activities of the Spirit Ancestors and their mythic connections with specific areas in the land. Song cycles — made up of series of different songs — formed a collective repository of sacred knowledge, each song recounting special events in the saga of Creation, and at times incorporating cryptically encoded 'secret' information within the ceremonial performances.

In Aboriginal Australia, prior to European contact, music varied considerably across the continent and, like the languages, although sharing common structural characteristics, there were differences in dialect. From what is now known, the songs of the Pintupi,[3] for example, and those of the 'Pitjantjatjara, Antakarinja, Wongkanguru, Arabana and Kokata-speaking peoples of northern South Australia, are structurally similar in almost all respects, having differences only in such features as vocal range and tone quality.'[4]

The word most commonly used by the Pitjantjatjara people from the north-west of South Australia, for example, to describe music is *inma* which is a broad-based term encompassing the entire spectrum of song and music, dance and design. The traditional usage of this word, 'apart from simply referring to ceremony or the fact that a song is to be performed, include "good" *inma*, "bad" or "unreliable" *inma* performances, an exceedingly sacred and secret ceremony, or a ceremony with a "false front" (*inma ngunti*)'.[5] The latter are songs which are taught to children in the camp and which also have behind them deeper meanings and contexts relating to secret ritual and ceremony. 'The word is also used to define the small unit of musical structure — the "small song". This is called *inma tjukutjuku. Inma* does not exist without the Dreaming which is its source.'[6]

A song line or Dreaming track consists of many 'small songs' recounting one long Creation myth. And, as we have

Island Corroboree, Clarke Island, Sydney.

indicated, Australian Aboriginal music is very much music of the land. In the same way that the Dreamtime Ancestors brought into being all forms of life and sustenance, so too was it considered necessary that the Ancestors be honoured through song and music, and the natural balance of Nature be respected and maintained — for thousands of years Aboriginal people have maintained their healthy survival upon the continent, carefully balancing the resources of native wildlife with what they took from the environment for food and shelter. Aboriginal people use their songs in all aspects of their lives: they are songs of power and vitality which renew the land by evoking and celebrating the spiritual bond which continues to exist between the Ancestral Beings and all created forms. So an important ceremonial function of song and music generally is to 'sing the health' of the land — and this responsibility is shared by all the women and men who have taken on the custodial role of preserving the sacred traditions within their respective communities.

Both women and men have their own musical knowledge, and also their own ritual

expressions and secret ceremonies which are particular to them. It is also true that in many groups some public ceremonial functions may be performed by men, women and children collectively. However, it is said that while in the past senior tribal men held authority over the most powerful songs, more recently this role has passed to the women who, throughout Australia, have assumed custodial responsibility of the ancient song maps known as the 'big songs' or 'history songs' of the Spirit Ancestors, as well as passing on those songs known as 'little histories' which have been composed by human beings in a more recent time frame.[7] Because the songs of power are held only by those who have received the appropriate initiations, they are generally held by the senior Law women and men, who have attained great rank and respect within their groups, and the songs can only be performed and thus transmitted by those who have this authority. A crucial factor in the transmission of the 'history songs' and their accompanying ritual practices was the strict observance of a high degree of accuracy in their commitment to memory. The sacred trust of the Dreamtime knowledge depended on this accuracy, this commitment to oral culture, and its continued transmission to future generations.

In these ways the most secret or sacred versions of the community's songs, or inside/outside stories, are guarded by the senior initiated Law women and men, while more open, or public, versions of the songs are available for the community as a whole. Some of these more general songs are also used as teaching stories for children. In this sense it is meaningful to distinguish between 'closed' and 'open' ceremonies within each community. In most groups the most senior person holds that status precisely because she or he is 'the person knowing many songs — the wise one'.[8]

In many parts of Australia there are songs that are exclusively either for women or for men, and it is believed that for a woman to hear a man's song in a sacred ceremony, or vice versa, could cause illness or death. For this reason, Aboriginal songs which have been made available to the general public are 'open' songs which are neither initiatory 'business' nor gender-specific and which are more in the genre of entertainment or teaching songs.

SONG LEADERS

In Aboriginal cultures, the element of song may be considered the most central aspect of any given musical performance because, although songs may be performed by themselves, it would be inconceivable for dances or ceremonial rituals to be performed without songs. Aboriginal peoples everywhere believe that when songs are sung properly, and in the correct ceremonial context, they tap into the creative power of the Dreamtime and revitalise the land and its inhabitants. As a consequence, because songs have such potency, they have to be sung by people who have this authority. These people are the song leaders and other specialist singers who have been chosen by the group for this role.

In both the women's and men's ceremonies the song leader is normally the senior custodian of the land. Generally speaking, each song begins with the song leader singing alone for a few seconds, with other members of the singing group subsequently joining in. Following the introductory sequence from the song leader, the other singers will usually sing in unison and follow the rhythm that has been established. If someone makes a mistake or begins to sing in a way that may weaken the performance, the more experienced singers will usually drown out the errors through the intensity of their own singing.

Opposite: *Endunga* by the eminent artist, the late Emily Kame Kngwarreye, an Anmatyerre woman from the Northern Territory. Courtesy of Coventry Gallery.

Wagilag Sisters by Philip Gudthaykudthay, a Llyagalawumirri man, who lives at Ramingining in central Arnhem Land. The Wagilag Sisters is a major creation song line or song cycle which underpins core religious practice in central Arnhem Land. The story and ceremony are associated with ensuring the continuation of the cycles of Nature. Also featured in this image is Yurlunggur (also known as Wititj), the giant python. Courtesy of Coo-ee Aboriginal Art.

The ability of the song leader is obviously central to the success of each performance, but in addition to having proven musical ability the song leader also has to have the ritual status to perform the task in the first instance. Nevertheless, distinctions may also be made about a person being a 'good' or a 'fine' singer, or having a 'strong' or 'light' tongue. Generally, for song leaders to be respected within their communities they must combine a profound knowledge of the myths with the charismatic ability to convey a feeling of reverence and enthusiasm through the musical performance itself.

The song leader has to be perfectly familiar with all the song texts and also has to know all their meanings and the correct sequence of the song series. This in itself is a considerable feat of memory, of oral culture, and the exact learning of lengthy song cycles is a process that usually takes many years to perfect. Young accompanists may need to listen several times before they are able to grasp even the basic details of the words, rhythm and melody lines, as they follow the song leader. There is also the possibility that the younger performers will often be quite unfamiliar with certain words or expressions used in the song cycles because these may be cryptic or secret references known only to a person who 'holds the knowledge'. Those who have not been initiated are not allowed to request further information about these particular references. Apart from the more general teaching stories for young children, learning of mythic material occurs only in the experiential ritual context. Also, knowledge has to be earned, it is not a given right as is generally the expectation in western cultures.

Another consideration is the sheer logistical structure of the larger song cycles. As we have said, traditional Aboriginal cultures are oral and the song texts must be memorised, which is formidable in itself. Among the Alyawarra people, who live north-east of Alice Springs, the song series in the *Agharringa* repertoire sometimes contain over a hundred individual songs, each one requiring technical mastery as well as forming part of an exact sequence. Meanwhile, the north-east Arnhem Land *kunapipi* ritual cycle includes 129 songs, the Djan'kawu fertility song cycle from Yirrkala contains 188 songs, and the related Miliningimbi cycle — which describes the journey of the Djan'kawu Beings to Balbanara — contains 264 songs.[9] It seems likely that the rhythmic structure of the song cycles also serves as a focusing device and helps the singers remember the correct sequence for each song. Even so, the feats of memory, of oral culture required are highly impressive.

Some of the individual songs in a cycle may be quite short — lasting perhaps only 30 seconds or so. These are the 'small songs', and usually they describe different locations in the journeys of the Spirit Ancestors. In a sense these songs are brief musical 'maps' which provide a context for the sequence of the song cycle. The longer and more substantial songs, on the other hand, contain much more specific mythic content and are intended to evoke in the

listeners' minds a complete sense of the immanence of the Spirit Ancestors and their active and ongoing relationship with the group. The most important songs are sometimes referred to as 'business' — and include 'big' songs — because they embody the spiritual principles of the Law and, by their very nature, are central to the community's sacred traditions.

Men's ceremony performed at Yuelamu community, Mount Allen, Northern Territory.

DANCE

Obviously dance is a central part of ritual and ceremony and cannot really be separated out from it. It is interconnected with music as a form of creative expression and continues to play an important part in the lives and culture of all Aboriginal people. Even in those areas where the colonising effects of white settlement meant that some ceremonies might be lost, no Aboriginal celebration would ever be performed without dance. In Aboriginal cultures, dance is often a 'pantomimic' interpretation of a major mythic event and some dances are linked into series which, like song cycles, may extend for several days and nights. Usually dance sequences of this type build up to a climax which is exciting and leaves a strong and lasting impact upon all who have participated.

The most common word associated with Aboriginal dance events is *corroboree*, which means a 'dance' or 'ceremony'. It is thought that the word itself may come from the language

Women's ceremony or
corroboree at Yuelamu
community, Mount Allen,
Northern Territory.

of the Eora people who used to live in the region around Sydney, but it has now passed into English usage as a word to describe all public Aboriginal ceremonies and entertainments involving singing and dancing.

There is a difference between dancing as an entertainment and dancing in ritual to express the spiritual themes of a myth. An Aboriginal ceremonial dancer is always fully aware of the dignity which is appropriate to such a performance and sacred dance is not treated lightly. However, this is not to say that public rituals lack excitement or energetic expression as well. A dramatic turn to a dance ceremony may take place, for example, when large heaps of dry grass are set ablaze, illuminating the dancers' bodies around the fire. The buffalo dances on Melville Island are characterised by lively leaping movements and vigorous stamping, and provide an exciting spectacle for both the onlooker and the participant.

As there are many terms to indicate different types of singing, so there are for dancing. In South Australia the key word for both female and male dancing activity is *pakani*, meaning 'rising'. There are also a number of specific technical terms which can apply to either male or female dance steps, for example: 'for quivering the thighs and knees; for stamping the feet; for dancing, carrying ceremonial objects; for the jumping motion performed by the women, which leaves continuous tracks in the sand'. There are also descriptive terms for other bodily movements such as 'head down on one side when dancing'.[10]

Dancing may be performed singly or in groups, and there are times when members of the audience may also participate. Children may be allowed to join in — a girl with the women, a boy with the men — and it is not uncommon to see a baby asleep in its mother's arms as she sways gently to the dance rhythms. Although there are always exceptions, Aboriginal women tend to dance in a more reflective and less obtrusive way, while the men often bring more physical energy and theatrics to their performances.

Dancing often precedes and closes major ceremonies, like initiation, and at these times the dancers will also be painted up with the appropriate insignia for the occasion. Whether these insignia are secret or non-secret might vary from place to place, but often the body paint designs are considered to be part of the sacred regalia which are held in trust by the custodians of the particular myth that is being performed. Sometimes dancers wear impressive conical headdresses made of down feathers and twine and also carry ceremonial objects in their hands — but once again, these elements are generally appropriate for a closed ceremony rather than a public performance.

In some parts of Aboriginal Australia, dancers may also dance with decorated or incised boards held above their heads. An example of this is provided by the *Krill Krill* rituals, which more recently have been associated with the beautiful ochre paintings of the internationally renowned Kimberley artist Rover Thomas, (Joolama) of the Kukatja-Wangakajunga people. However, the early *Krill Krill* dance boards were not painted by Rover Thomas himself but by his mother's brother, Paddy Jaminji, and they were used as icons held over the dancers' heads in public ceremonies, or *palga*. There are times, though, when the contents of a dance board may be restricted, and not available for all to see. Sometimes in ritual dance performances which involve both men and women, but which are partially restricted, for example to women and children, there may be a short sequence where the women dancers would have to lower their heads and not look at the dance board insignia being presented in that part of the dance

Senior Law woman Matingali (Mati) Bridget Matjital, *right*, of the Ngarti people, and Anna Voigt.

Opposite:
Nakarra Nakarra Dreaming by senior Law woman Matingali (Mati) Bridget Matjital of the Ngarti people. The incident depicted by Matingali in this painting concerns two of the Nakarra Nakarra women — a mother and her daughter — who went hunting the Wallupanta snake. They searched and searched, but the snake had gone underground to a site called Tarlapunta, where it still lives today in a large claypan. These events are commemorated by local women in ceremony. Courtesy of Manungka Manungka Women's Association.

— and the opposite would pertain if women's symbols were being presented to a group containing both female and male performers. Sometimes, too, a senior Law woman or man may have a dream in which new songs or dances are presented to them as a revelation, and they may wish to share these with other members of their community. However, these dream revelations are considered to be the activity of Spirit Ancestors. The source of all creativity is the Ancestral Beings — human beings are transmitters or agents but not creators. Again such song and dance sequences would be 'closed' if they contained elements that were considered sacred.

Matingali Bridget Matjital Napanangka (affectionately known as Mati), Nararti Law woman, talked with the author, Anna Voigt, about how as a child she learned ceremonial dancing and song:

MM: We watch 'im dancing, you know. Dancing. Mother and granny, auntie. All bin dancing that Nakarra Nakarra Dreaming. Proper important. Long, long time before we never bin born yet, nothing. All the women bin keep 'im [the Nakarra Nakarra Law]. Nungarrayai [Mati's grandmother] and Napaltjarri and Nangala, Napurulla. Alright, we bin born. Little bit, we bin grown big. Now we watching all the dancing. Granny too. Granny and mother. . .We bin watching. We never bin leave 'im culture. Teaching culture. We bin learn [from] watching, you know, dancing.

AV: When did you do the dancing?

MM: Dancing little bit big one. Before this one [indicates breasts]. Before got milk. Dancing now alright. Mother take 'im dance.

AV: So you were watching, watching, watching, and then when you were a big girl?

MM: Big girl go work [as domestic at Sturt Creek Station]. Still thinking for ceremony, for Nakarra Nakarra. Still thinking. . .All been singing too, there. Singing and painting [body painting]. . .

AV: So, did your mother and grandmother say when you could dance?

MM: Yeah. They say, Now you can dance we dance 'im. We look at 'im mother. My mother dancing, my granny too. [Mati followed on behind.]

MM: Yeah. And ochre. All around ochre.

AV: Did you paint up [ceremonial body painting]?

MM: Yeah.

AV: And the little girls, are they painted up too?

MM: Yeah, we paint 'im too. Carmen [one of Mati's grandchildren, a two-year-old granddaughter]. Yeah, I teaching that one. [Mati claps.] He [she] gotta stop la [with] me. He gotta stop my grannie [granddaughter].

AV: Carmen is two years old and she is already painted up?

MM: Napurulla, Napurulla. From my son Tjakamarra. I teach 'im.

AV: So, the teaching starts the beginning of a child's life?

MM: Dancing.

AV: And singing?

MM: [Claps] . . .

AV: . . .And the dances are particular song lines. You teach your children the song lines.
Are there different song lines for the different children or the same?

MM: Same. Sometimes Mina-Mina, sometimes Nakarra Nakarra.

AV: Everybody shares the song lines?

MM: Yeah, just two.

AV: And do you teach all the different parts of the song lines or the same parts?

MM: Same one. . .[With the little (*lampan*) ones, just one song, one dance is taught.]

AV: Because song lines are a big journey?

MM: Yeah. Little bit.

AV: A little bit at a time. It's beautiful. It's very *palya* [good].[11]

By way of summary, we can distinguish three different types of Aboriginal dance. There are
rituals and ceremonies which deal with the re-enactment of a sacred myth, and on these
occasions the structure of the ceremony, the musical accompaniment and the dancing are all
interdependent. Then there are individual or collective dance routines and movements which
may be associated with particular songs but which are not considered 'sacred' or 'secret' —
these may be performed at public ceremonies like *corroborees* or in other 'open' events. And
finally there are contemporary dance sequences which have been choreographed by individual
performance artists and Aboriginal dance companies. All of these dance forms are a vital aspect
of the Aboriginal experience and, in their own distinctive ways, are a profound expression of
the innate spirituality of the Aboriginal traditions.

Opposite: *Digging Stick Dreaming* by Warlpiri artist Maggie Napangardi. This painting depicts part of an epic song line journey undertaken by female Ancestor Spirits in the Dreamtime. The Digging Sticks are represented by four black verticle lines on the left hand side of the painting. The ancestral women are called Digging Stick and their journey begins from Mina Mina (Dreaming track) and continues through a number of sacred sites, represented by circles where the women danced and performed their ceremonies. The women did many things in the course of their journey, one of which was to collect *Ngalyipimalu* (Snake Vine) to fasten their *coolamuns* (or *coolamons*) to their hips while they collected food. These lines are represented by the snake-like lines running vertically through the painting. Courtesy of Kimberley Art.

Game won't increase unless you perform their ceremonies.

That's what we believe...

By singing and dancing the kangaroo ceremony, say, we believe old

kangaroo — he'll breed more. He likes to hear his songs.

That way he feels he's important. So he goes off and makes more

kangaroos. Which means your people have plenty of tucker to eat.

That's why ceremony is so important. It keeps the land alive.

Without ceremony the land soon dies...

The land needs us just as much as we need it.[1]

Chapter Five

RITUAL AND CEREMONY

Each ceremony brings people together for a shared purpose which is important and central to their lives — so by its very nature it is a wonderful way of bonding a community. Also, in virtually all ceremonies, everyone has a place and a role to play, so all in a community feel a fundamental sense of belonging.

The act of singing is vital to the potency of a ceremonial performance and touches every member of the community. The selection of participants for each individual ceremony is also a way of acknowledging the status and distinctive roles of individual members of the society. The ritual owners of a mythic cycle are responsible for the performance of ceremonies and songs associated with it.

In most groups there is a specific role of 'manager' — this person has a social obligation to help 'stage manage' the ceremony and look after the land where the ceremonies are held. In Arnhem Land this role is called *junggayi* and among the Warlpiri, *kurdungurlu*. Here the children of the women of a particular patrilineal descent group are both entitled and obliged to become the ritual managers for their mothers and their mother's brothers. They have to learn the spiritual traditions of their mother's people — at a level that is appropriate to their age and gender — and also inspect the ceremonial lands to ensure that there have been no unauthorised intruders. The ritual 'managers' learn about the ceremonial use of ochre and down feathers, and prepare the sacred ground for the actual ceremony when it is to take place.

THE BORA GROUND

In some parts of Australia the meeting place for sacred ceremonies is known as a *bora* ground or *bora* ring — especially in New South Wales, southern Queensland and the Gippsland area of Victoria. The word *bora* is a Kamilaroi term which describes the fur-string belt — the 'belt of manhood' — which was worn traditionally by men initiated into the secret cult of Biami. However, the term *bora* has now acquired a more general application for the location of both women's and men's ceremonies and is widely used in this way, although there are also other names for these ceremonial grounds, like *buhl* (Bandjalung), *buurrbang* (Wiradjuri) or *bungul* (Datiwuy).

Traditionally, in most *bora* grounds two large circles — one twice as big as the other — were dug in the Earth and connected by a straight or 'wavy' pathway which always ran in an east–west direction to symbolise the rising and setting of the sun within the cycle of each person's individual life. Trees adjoining the sacred site would often be carved with totemic insignia and motifs, and with depictions of Spirit Ancestors like the Rainbow Serpent.

With regard to the two *bora* circles inscribed upon the ground, 'in most areas the smaller circle symbolised the constant fertility of women, and the never-ending reproduction of human life, while the larger represented the eternal link of people and Nature in the broader cycle, or circle, of Creation'.[2] In some parts of Australia — especially in the east and south-east, the *bora* ring sites were used over a long period of ceremonial history and were permanent structures on the ground, whereas in northern and central Australia they were created afresh for each initiation ceremony.

CEREMONIAL PERFORMANCES

As a general principle it can be said that ceremonial performances are restricted to people of a certain standing, or status, within the group. Certain ceremonies might be open, for example, only to senior women (adult women with two or more children) or in other instances reserved only for senior men. Some group members would specialise in singing, others in dancing, and if the ritual had a particular healing emphasis there would be those who would help focus the revitalising powers of the ceremony towards those who were ailing in the community. Other 'open' ceremonies might be available to all members of the group, including children. *Corroborees*, for example, are always considered to be 'open' or public ceremonies. Children are not admitted to closed adult ceremonies but may, on occasion, have their own ceremonies. Among the Alyawarra people the children of the Urriltja country have a ceremony called *puratja* which is held when a child catches its first goanna or blue-tongue lizard.[3]

A typical ceremonial performance might begin with general singing within the camp to signal that a certain ritual or 'business' was about to commence. Then participants would move to the formal ceremonial setting which would have areas prepared for both the dancers and the singers, including temporary shelters where dancers could prepare their ceremonial attire and decoration. Fires would normally act as a barrier between the dancers and the singers, and would also be used to evoke a sense of ritual drama and excitement in the performance.

When we are considering the role of song and ceremony within the group there can be no doubt that the most important function of a ceremonial performance is to draw upon the sacred power of the Dreamtime as a living force. There are songs that are associated with all

aspects of life — with birth, with initiation, with love and marriage, with food gathering, with conflict resolution, with healing and with death — and these are always sung and performed in an appropriate context. In addition to this, when a person sings a song in a ceremonial context it is considered to be effective in bringing about an actual change in circumstances — for the person or the object for whom the song is intended, has been 'sung'. Songs and ceremonies are powerful and enlivening — they have a magical and transformative potency, and provide a key for how one should live one's life within the sacred Law.

Aboriginal women are the nurturers of both the country and the people. As anthropologist Diane Bell says of Central Australian Aboriginal women:

Above: Ceremonial preparation — Yuelamu community at Mount Allen, Northern Territory.

Overleaf:
Tiwi Corroboree, Bathurst Island. Courtesy of Wildlight.

Opposite: Women's ceremony or *corroboree* at Yuelamu community, Mount Allen, Northern Territory.

...in ritual women emphasize their role as nurturers of people, land and relationships. Through their *yawulyu* (land-based ceremonies) they nurture land; through their health and curing rituals they resolve conflict and restore social harmony, and through *yilpinji* (emotional management rituals) they manage emotions. Thus in women's rituals their major responsibilities in the areas of love, land and health fuse in the nurturance motif with its twin themes of the 'growing up' of people and land and the maintenance of harmonious relations between people and country.[4]

This concept of nurturance is very different to that of western cultures and is central to Aboriginal spiritual beliefs and practices. When Aboriginal women dance with their sacred ritual boards and with their hands cupped towards the sky they are helping to 'grow up' their sacred lands. This concept of nurturance is also directly linked to the Dreamtime Creation and the ways that women create and grow up country and kin. Actual childbirth and personal motherhood, although important personal experience, is seen more in terms of connections with Spirit Ancestors in the larger stream of eternal creation. The women's rituals — their *yawulyu* (or *awelye*) and *yilpinji* — also encompass the ritual domains of both men and women, for in both types of rituals there is a celebration of the central values of the society and a recognition that society must be maintained in accordance with Dreamtime Law.

The Kaytej women at Warribri in Central Australia conduct *yawulyu* ceremonies which are linked to three major themes — land, love and health. These are all a part of the women's *Tjukurrpa* (the Dreamtime) heritage and are generally held about once a week.

While the women are preparing the items for ritual, and painting the symbolic map designs on their bodies, they sing quietly and reflect on the Dreamtime traditions evoked by their ritual. The body painting part of the ritual is a group activity which allows those without much expertise to acquire the knowledge necessary to apply the symbolic designs. During this 'painting up' activity the variety of songs, rhythms and symbolic procedures is much more extensive than that which occurs in the more public ceremonies.

On the day of the *yawulyu*, after all the ritual paraphernalia have been gathered and the body painting is complete, most of the women move to their dancing place and sit facing in a westerly direction. Some now begin to sing the songs which call all the other participants to come. A fire is kept alight during the ritual and the same pile of ashes retained and reignited on subsequent ritual occasions.

A *yawulyu* performance for a specific purpose can be comparatively short but incorporates activities linked symbolically to 'country' on both the mother's and father's side — *kurdungurlu* (managers) and *kirda* (owners) respectively. These include details of particular locations within the country in each case, Dreamings owned by both sides of the family, and songs relating to both. During the ritual, performers associated with the two descent groups also sing and dance using ritual boards which contain secret motifs, and in this way re-affirm the kinship divisions which were taught to them by the Spirit Ancestors.

Some of the *kirda* and *kurdungurlu* — who exist in a complementary relationship — are seated and sing songs relating to Dreaming sites while other performers 'plant' the ritual boards in different positions, locating each Dreaming as they do so. The boards are then treated reverently in terms of their association with different 'countries' and may be addressed through kinship terms like mother, father or auntie. In this manner both the ritual relationship to country and the deep emotional personal tie to country are given expression. After they have been positioned, each ritual board becomes the focus of the ceremony as the Dreamtime travels of the Ancestors are re-enacted. Performers from both the mother's side and the father's side then sing and dance. The dancing itself includes symbolically encoded information, and only initiated members would know the meanings underlying this aspect of the performance.

> After the dancing concludes the women sing the Dreaming into the ground and visitors would be expected to leave at this point. The participants then smooth over all traces on the ground where the ritual boards were located, throw dirt on the ground to nullify any remaining power, and rub the boards onto their bodies to absorb their ritual power.[5]

The transference of power is extremely dangerous and in certain contexts, such as in women's resolution of conflict rituals, can constitute the most sacred moments of women's *yawulyu*. Once stripped, the sacred boards are carefully replaced in the storehouse specifically used to house sacred objects.

Both present-day dreams and songs — indeed all aspects of creative activity — are seen as emanating from the activities of the Spirit Ancestors and then flowing through human agents. Only the Ancestors can create — their Aboriginal descendants operate as conduits for their creative powers and are to be seen to act as responsible custodians of Ancestral Law. On a cultural level one could say that little has changed, but at a more superficial level much may seem to have changed over time. However, these changes do not in themselves indicate any alteration of direction or intention of the Ancestors — for that is bound by the Law. But because the Law is only made known through human agents, over generations, it seems inevitable that changes would occur. And although each song, dance and symbolic design may have an individual rendering to a certain degree, the fact that each rendering is underwritten and is a re-affirmation of Dreamtime Law virtually guarantees that no individual can lay claim to being an inspired author. Also with the *kumanjayi* (no name) system, where all of the 'belongings' — including the name - of a deceased person are removed from the living, only the legacy of the Ancestral Beings remains within the society — to be renewed with each generation.[6]

THE DJAN'KAWU DUA NARA

The major Djan'kawu Creation myth referred to in chapter two, underwrites and gives traditional sanction to the performance of the rituals known as the *dua nara* of the Yolngu people of Arnhem Land. *Dua* is the name of the moiety primarily concerned with this myth and its symbols and rituals. Its opposite moiety, the *Jiritja*, has a counterpart in the *jiritja nara*, sanctioned by Laintjung, an Ancestral Being. The Djan'kawu Ancestral heroes of the *Dua* moiety arrived by sea, whereas the Ancestors of the *Jiritja* moiety, such as Laintjing, came from the land.

The Djan'kawu, Laintjing, his son Banaitja and the Wauwalak, as we have said, are the principal Ancestral Beings in eastern Arnhem Land who have instituted religious belief, ritual and behaviour. However, the Djan'kawu Sisters and Brother and the Djan'kawu religious cult is, to the Aboriginal people themselves, more important than other religious cults in that region. The cult appears not to have absorbed alien elements and thus has remained more 'purely traditional' than, for example, the later well-known Wauwalak cycle which provides the basis for the *djunggawon*, *kunapipi* — discussed later in this chapter — and *ngurlmag* rituals.[7]

The Djan'kawu myth expresses the fundamental idea of the ebb and flow of the tides in the spring floods, in the Dreamtime and in the present day, and how this seasonally brings forth new life. With each new season and with each new generation a species is reborn. The myth is thus primarily and intimately concerned with fertility and with all the elements that enable the continuity of all that exists to Aboriginal people. To bring forth fertility in all that lives is of prime importance so the sequential rhythm of the seasons must be assured. The desire to maintain, or attain, seasonal fertility is expressed symbolically in the myth and accompanying songs and physically in totemic form. The main focus is on the primary human drives of sex (in the wider sense) and food — both of which are necessary for survival of the species. By re-enacting the primal birth of their Ancestors the *Dua* moiety clan affirm their sense of group continuity.

The perpetually pregnant Djan'kawu Sisters are Fertility Mothers who have given birth to the '*rangga* folk' — who are the Ancestors of present-day Aboriginal people. The sacredness of Woman is emphasised with full recognition that the survival of the group is primarily dependent on the fertility of the female. Thus motherhood is given its due honour in this culture. That virile man is biologically necessary for insemination of the female is also given recognition in the myth and rituals — acknowledging the interdependent roles of female (maternity) and male (paternity) in the survival of the people.

The great *dua nara* of the Djan'kawu religious cult are performed solely by members of the *Dua* moiety and are revelatory in character. They are performed by the *Dua* initiated men over several days, although their preparations can take many weeks. Initially the men go out to the ceremonial ground and prepare the sacred objects, which in this area are called *rangga*. These are wooden poles and posts which have various symbolic references. They are kept hidden in waterholes or in the muddy banks and must be redecorated for the ceremonies.

Periodically, those to be initiated as novices have their chests painted with sacred clan designs to formally contract ritual obligations and reciprocity. These designs must not be removed but left to fade naturally. The women also have an important part to play in these initial ceremonies. They make long feathered strings which are then ritually stolen from them by the men. This relates directly to a central incident in the myth which tells how once the ritual objects and ceremonies were owned by women, the creator Djan'kawu Sisters — Bildjiwuraru and Miralaidj — but were stolen by the men they had created. All of the lengthy preparations are accompanied by songs and invocations.

When the preliminaries to the ceremony of this myth are over, the ritual ceremonial ground is prepared and a shelter is erected. It now becomes a sacred area in which the Djan'kawu will be manifest. The shelter symbolises the womb of the two sisters of Djan'kawu. The first dances relate to the rising and falling of the surf and the sound of the sea and they symbolise the Djan'kawu's paddling across the sea to Port Bradshaw.

Throughout the dancing and singing of the song cycle, invocations are made which connect the power of Djan'kawu with those creating the ceremony.

Much of the latter part of the ceremony dramatises the stealing of the sacred objects from the two Sisters. The final part of this sequence comes with the men coming to the main camp holding flaming torches. This is a symbolic reference to the Sisters believing their sacred dilly bags containing the *rangga*, sacred objects, were destroyed by fire — before they discovered that they had really been stolen by the men. The cycle of rituals and ceremonies concludes with a ritual bathing in which the men, followed by the women and children, dance down to the beach and plunge into the water. This may symbolise the Djan'kawu returning to Bralgu, their island home.

Afterwards there follows the ritual eating of sacred cycad nut bread which has been made by the women. The eating of the bread creates a sacred bond of friendship between the participants: they become as one.[8]

THE UBAR, MARAIIN AND KUNAPIPI

Although considered less important than the Djan'kawu *dua nara*, another interesting and significant ceremonial cycle is performed by the Gunwinggu people (or Kunwinjku), whose traditional lands are in western Arnhem Land. The Gunwinggu trace descent matrilineally and their society is divided into moieties, semi-moieties and subsections: these divisions are also symbolically associated with many natural species. The basic moieties are called *Madgu* and *Ngaraidgu*, and each Gunwinggu person is born into either one or the other. However, because Gunwinggu society is matrilineal, a child is always born into his mother's moiety. The semi-moieties and subsections are also matrilineal.

Like all Aboriginal groups the Gunwinggu have a strong and ongoing spiritual relationship with their Spirit Ancestors and believe they derive their spiritual power or *djang* from them. However, *djang* can manifest in different ways. Sacred plant or animal *djang* — inherent within natural species created during the Dreamtime — is able at different times to undergo various forms of metamorphosis. The original *djang* then leaves its mark on each new species in turn. Ronald and Catherine Berndt provide an example:

> A *djang* which turned into an animal or bird or *some* other creature left in *every* representative of that particular species, a living, observable example of its original form, and of its character and its spirit; the Rainbow is the *original* Ngaljod [or Ngalyod] snake, and with the same relevance to man as she always had.[9]

When one considers the close relationship between the Gunwinggu people and a great range of natural species, and also their concept of *djang*, it is not surprising that many of their ceremonies are concerned with fertility, with the impact of the Spirit Ancestors on the land, and with the cyclic pattern of the seasons.

Apart from their mortuary ceremonies, the three major ritual cycles performed by the Gunwinggu (Kunwinjku) are the *ubar*, *maraiin* and *kunapipi* (or *gunabibi*). A dominant presence in each of them is the figure of the Mother, sometimes called 'Old Woman' — in Aboriginal cultures this is a term of respect for age rather than being a derogatory term. For the Gunwinggu people Old Woman is essentially a Fertility Mother,

Opposite: *Luma Luma Story* by the late Bobby Nganjmira, a Gunwinggu (or Kunwinjku) man from western Arnhem Land. Luma Luma, a giant, was an Ancestor who came from across the sea and terrorised the people before giving them the very important *Maraiin* rituals. Courtesy Coo-ee Aboriginal Art.

responsible for creating many of the natural species found on both land and sea. She is also the Spirit Ancestor of present-day human beings. In her guise as Ngaljod or Yulunggul, the Rainbow Serpent, she is sometimes known as *gagag*, or mother's mother. At other times she is known as Waramurungundji.

According to several myths it was women who first had possession of the *ubar* ritual which was later stolen from them by the men. Aboriginal women sometimes call the Fertility Mother in *ubar* ritual Ngaldjorlbu: 'She is like Ngaljod, she looks like a woman and carries a digging stick. . .' A digging stick is the most important tool of Aboriginal women. They also say that the *ubar* is 'a Mother ritual for all of us. . .she is our Mother. . .all of us everywhere, dark skin or light skin, people of every place and of different languages — we all call her Mother, our true Mother, who made herself *djamun* [taboo, set apart] for us.'[10]

With regard to the second ceremonial group, the *maraiin* rituals, Gunwinggu tradition maintains that two male spirits, Laradjeidja (*Jiritja* moiety) and Gundamara (*Dua* moiety) created them. Lumaluma the giant is an important ancestral being who also instituted the *maraiin* ceremonial ritual. Like the two male Creator-Spirits, he also came from the east and travelled overland, accompanied beneath the Earth by Ngaljod the Rainbow. (There are certain parallels here with the eastern Arnhem Land Djan'kawu myth cycle.)

To take part in the *maraiin* rituals the candidate must first have participated in the earlier *ubar* rituals, and after his first *maraiin* experience a Gunwinggu man may then take a wife. Even so, *maraiin* ceremonial activities will continue throughout his life. The rituals are very varied and so too are the ritual objects utilised in them. Between performances these sacred objects are wrapped in paperbark bundles called *dudji*, and carefully stored.

The third of the myth–ritual sequences, the *kunapipi* (*gunabibi*) is very widespread in the Northern Territory and has reasonably similar procedures, sacred objects and ritual expressions. As in the *ubar* mythology, women first owned the *kunapipi* ritual. Ronald Berndt explains that sections of the story resemble the well-known Wawilak (Warwilag or Wauwalak) Sisters corpus of myths in eastern Arnhem Land, but from recent written accounts it seems to be recognised that incidents in the rituals are underpinned by events from the Wawilak cycle relating to 'women's business'. The Berndts have written a fascinating account of what happens when a *kunapipi* ritual takes place:

> When a *kunapipi* sequence is about to commence, messengers (*gagawar*) go out to summon visitors. A Gunwinggu performance is most likely to be instigated and directed by visiting southern people. Other visitors come to be initiated as novices or to have sections of the ritual revealed to them. The sacred ground which is the centre of the rites varies in shape and is called the *ganala*. It is a trench two to three feet deep, symbolizing the uterus of the Mother, or Ngaljod (or Yulunggul) the Rainbow Snake, or both. On the inner walls of the *ganala*, snake designs are incised. It is said that in some cases a *nanggaru* hole is dug on the sacred ground, representing a sacred waterhole and also the Mother's uterus.

> The distinctive long-drawn calling begins, and men bringing novices (*walg*) come up to the sacred ground: 'The Mother is calling them, they will be swallowed by the Snake.' Simultaneously, bullroarers are swung — usually the female ones, the

mumana (or Ngalmamuna, the Mother's name, a non-secret word) or 'Mother one'. The bullroarer is also called her *mai* (or 'meat'), like the Rainbow and its ritual representation is the *jelmalandji* [the *kunapipi* ritual poles]. Its sound, as it is swung, is the voice of the Snake, the female Yulunggul (Ngaljod): 'She comes out, she calls them, she talks, she goes with them to the sacred ground!'

There are three major ritual song divisions: *djamala, gudjiga* — which is traditionally performed at full moon — and *warimulunggul.* The first covers ritual sequences centering on the *ganala* (the sacred poles representing the uterus) and the *jelmalandji* (the ritual poles) and the instruction of young novices. The second conventionally includes ritual coitus, symbolising fertility, but the songs may be sung without that accompaniment. The third covers all *kunapipi* singing and ritual carried out in cooperation with women or in the main camp: all *warimulunggul* singing is 'open' or public.

On the sacred ground, postulants dance out various sequences relating to creatures mentioned in the songs. They emerge from where they have been hidden, move toward the *ganala* and enter it — they have been 'swallowed by the Rainbow' and have 'entered the Mother's uterus': they are sung over, and the cry of *Kunapipila* rings out! Before they witness such acts, novices have sweat rubbed on their eyes, and this is done afterward to the actors themselves.

A long series of rites follows, until the time comes to erect the *jelmalandji* emblems. The larger emblem is *Jiritja*, the smaller emblem *Dua*. At first the *jelmalandji* is erected near the *Jiritja* shelter: *Dua* men are led before it and embrace it and throw bunches of leaves in front of it. Throughout the night, women call from the camp. Food, prepared by the women, is brought up at intervals: it is sacred cycad-palm food.

Then follows a possum dancing series. Later, they all red-ochre themselves, surround the *jelmalandji* and push it down. All participants are now painted over with blood, on a base of red ochre mixed with termite mound. Young novices, lying in the grass some little distance away, are seized and also painted with blood. Symbolically, this means that all of them have been inside the belly of the Snake. While this is happening, ritual crying continues, along with the swinging of bullroarers. All the men now wear white headbands, *maralbibi.* They leave for the main camp, where a *djebalmandji* (or *djebanbani*) has been erected on the outskirts. This is two forked posts with a connecting ridge pole, covered with branches. This is a special shade associated mythically with flying foxes, and it can also represent the Mother's uterus. Singing begins, and women come to the *djebalmandji* and lie down around it covered with mats and blankets. Men dance around them. Then the women begin to leave, and men continue to dance as the novices are brought out from under the branches and go away with the women.

Finally comes an exchange of sweat, and more ritual calling. Tabu-ed food is given to the participants. Just as in the *maraiin,* married men are not permitted to sleep with their wives yet or share food with them — not until their paint rubs off entirely — because Ngaljod would resent it. The novices camp together on one side of the main camp. About two days later, all the participants and onlookers, men and women as well as novices, are painted with fat and red ochre, with body designs of female and male Ngaljod and her eggs. Payments are made to the *kunapipi* directors and an exchange of goods takes place between visitors and local people — which are then redistributed within the communities.[11]

The myth on which the *kunapipi* rituals is based is very long, and women's and men's versions of the rituals cover unusually large stretches of country. Interestingly though, not all aspects of the myth are actually enacted ceremonially by the Gunwinggu. References to fertility abound — the growing of vegetable and plant food and new grass shoots, the nesting of birds, the laying of eggs, and so on. At various times and places, in the course of their travels, the Ancestors perform parts of the *kunapipi* ritual for the 'new people' — the human beings — and also leave sacred objects behind. In all versions of the myth, Ngaljod, the Rainbow Snake, is an integral part of the *kunapipi* ritual.

A *kunapipi* ritual complex which immigrated to the Oenpelli (Gunbalanya) area of western Arnhem Land included 'protective magic' for women and men experiencing the rites for the first time. 'The spirit of a snake or a small parrot was sung into the back of their heads', so that it could warn them should anyone stealthily attempt to work sorcery[12] upon them or to spear them in the back.[13] Although the *kunapipi* has a certain fluidity its basic core remains constant, with much the same sacred objects, myths, songs and ritual sequences.

One of the details that the three rituals — *ubar*, *maraiin* and *kunapipi* — have in common is that in all three the men enter the Mother — in the shape of the sacred shade, the sacred ground, the *ganala*, and so on. At these times they are all symbolically within the Mother, and so by the time they later return to camp they are naturally 'reborn'. They acquire a new social status, and are acknowledged to have reached a new stage in their progression through life. Fully initiated men who have taken part are revitalised as well because in a very real sense they too have been in direct association with powerful elemental forces. Gunwinggu (Kunwinjku) men consider that one of their most important social roles is to protect themselves, and also their women and children, through careful performance of rituals which evoke and recreate the sagas of the Dreamtime. The women also have their own ceremonial acts, and as providers of sacred food assist in maintaining a ceremonial tradition which has continued in Gunwinggu society from distant times past.

Most of the 'big' rituals of the Gunwinggu — *ubar*, *lorrokon* (the mortuary rituals), *mangindjeg*, *maraiin* and *kunapipi* — emphasise fertility and the increase of natural species.

PERFORMING A RITUAL

The performance of a ritual is a symbolic action that has a specific end in mind. It is the outward expression of a myth, and has further meaning for social living either in the here and now of physical life or in ongoing spiritual existence. The belief in a ritual rests in the mythological events of the Dreamtime, though not all myths are enacted in ritual. Also a ritual action does not necessarily need a ceremonial setting.

Aboriginal peoples use ritual to symbolically recreate Dreamtime events in order to

Overleaf:
Corroboree. Courtesy of Wildlight.

establish and maintain contact with their Spirit Ancestors. In so doing, both the people and the Ancestors form a sacred pact to ensure the continuity of all life. Thus in essence, all sacred ritual is focused on life — for it is Spirit that gives life. Spiritual or ritual practice is the major integrating force of Aboriginal cultures and is relevant to all aspects of living as it is wholeheartedly believed that it is absolutely necessary for both physical and spiritual survival.

Ritual performances, then, can be grouped under a few broad categories. There are rituals that are strictly for women and rituals that are strictly for men, respectively called 'business'; rituals in which both women and men participate together in the same area, and rituals in which men play a major part at one site and women perform complementary actions at another site — either simultaneously or at a different time. Some of the rites which men perform in ceremonies closed to women, symbolically imitate certain physiological processes natural to women — as we have seen in the Djan'kawu *dua nara* and *kunapipi* rituals, for instance. Ceremony is considered a symbolical way for men to get in touch with the natural creative energies of woman. Subincision (the making of an incision in the urethra through the underside of the penis — connected to initiations specifically in the Western and Central Desert regions) is based on this analogy in that the blood flow down the thighs and onto the ground is like a woman's menstrual flow. Also in some areas circumcision is seen as the severing of the umbilical cord which symbolically severs a boy from his mother's influence. Related to these rituals are the various mythical accounts of women originally owning some of the most significant rituals and sacred objects which were stolen and taken control of by men. These sacred objects hold the title deeds to country.

THE ROM CEREMONY

In several regions of Australia, music and ceremony are used to formalise the territorial relationships between different Aboriginal groups. In north-eastern Arnhem Land the sacred song cycles which link different regions and communities are known as *manikay* — and through the song lines they may extend over substantial distances. Among the Anbarra people who live near the mouth of the Blyth River, there is a ceremony which is essentially an act of friendship, its main role being to celebrate good will and trade between different neighbouring groups. Known as the *Rom* (or *Marrajirri*), the ritual performance incorporates a cycle of *manikay* songs, accompanying dances and presentation of a ceremonial pole.

A *Rom* ceremonial relationship begins when a leading member of one community offers to trade goods with members of another group. Members of the recipient community then spend a number of months transforming a wooden pole into a beautifully decorated gift — the pole is carefully painted with ochre and embellished with specially chosen feathers, and embodies key aspects of the group's *manikay* song cycle and sacred symbols from their local clan mythology. In due course the group who have constructed the ceremonial *Rom* pole make a journey to the host community, who offer them gracious hospitality in return. After several days of singing and dancing, the visiting group hand over their *Rom* pole to the other group and are given food and gifts in return.

Among the Anbarra, *manikay* ceremonial performances include both women and men. Normally there is a male singer who accompanies himself with clapsticks, and also a *didjeridu* player. A group of men sing the songs while women dance at their side. In this ceremony singers must belong to the same moiety — either *Duwa* or *Yirricha* (*Dua* and *Jiritja* in Djan'kawu). Within each moiety in turn there are three clans, and these clans are custodians of different *manikay*. Among the Anbarra people, for example, members of one particular clan are guardians and performers of the Jambich (wild honey) *manikay* cycle which includes references to several Dreamings, among them King Brown Snake, White Cockatoo, Shark, Yam, North-west Monsoon, Conical Fishtrap and Marawal Spirit Men.[14]

The Jambich cycle includes numerous references to wild honey — a symbol of abundance and vitality ('. . .food overflows the dry trunk of Hollow Tree, Tree trunk filled to overflowing. . .'). *Manikay*s themselves are not confined to *Rom* ceremonies — they are also sung during male circumcision ceremonies, during mortuary rites, and around the campfires at night. The presentation of a *Rom* ceremonial pole to another community, though, is a special event and occurs much less often.

In the Beginning human beings were one with their totem —

man was yam, sugarbag, owl, kapok, fish, waterlily, turkey, emu or wallaby —

man was present in every kind of food...at first.

A person is inseparable from his totem.

Man and totem hold, guard and are bound by each other's life energies...

The totems were given by Wallanganda [Creator Being]

so that Aborigines would have no reason to fight for land or food.[1]

Chapter Six

TOTEM, KIN, FAMILY AND SURVIVAL

One way in which all Aboriginal peoples are linked to the sacred landscape is through their totemic bond with their Spirit Ancestors. The word 'totem' itself is not an ideal term to use in an Aboriginal context — it derives from a Native American Chippeway (Objibwa) term which has been translated as 'guardian spirit', and conceptually this does not capture the richness of the unique relationship Aboriginal people have with their Ancestors. Nevertheless, it is a word which is widely used today to describe aspects of Aboriginal spirituality, though 'Dreaming' is a preferable term.

TOTEM

Totems are Dreamings. In the Dreamtime human beings were one with their Dreaming — humankind, as Ngarinyin elder, David Mowaljarlai, has said, were first yams, ants, owls, particular fish, waterlilies, emus, kangaroos and so on. Totem beings, the creative Spirit Ancestors, then descended into the Earth at particular places or energised specific locations linked with a particular species. These *wunggud* or *djang* places are where those belonging to a particular totem or Dreaming go to activate the life force which ensures that a particular species continues on in Nature. Each totem, or Dreaming, and each individual person born in the country of that totem being, are inexorably connected, and she or he has an obligation to help continue the totemic species. Totems are a way of ordering the entire Universe and all the species who inhabit it. It is the Law which has passed down from the Dreamtime Ancestors which has made it so.

For all Aboriginal people the eternal bond between specific Spirit Ancestors, and particular sacred tracts of land linked to those Ancestors, is confirmed through initiation. When the individual is initiated into the mysteries of the group — including the sacred mythic knowledge associated with those sites — she or he becomes the custodian for that land, and subsequently acknowledges an ongoing obligation to reinforce that sacred bond through ceremonial observances which take place on the land itself. To this extent initiation is a key to understanding the very heart of totemism. By definition initiation opens the door to sacred knowledge — and for a person to be acknowledged as a custodian of the land is to have a special status conferred by the group as a whole.

Because there is always this spiritual link with the land — inherent from birth but confirmed through initiation — and because custodianship of land also brings with it the right to hunt and gather food within that designated territory, it is natural that an important feature of Aboriginal totemism is the special relationship with different plant and animal species that abound on that land, and which are mythically associated with it. As hunters and foragers, all Aboriginal peoples are literally sustained by the bounty of the Earth — by animals killed in the bush or through native plants and fruits gathered as bush tucker — but the concept of spiritual sustenance, which is central to the totemic idea, goes far beyond physical livelihood. For here we are dealing with the unique bond between Aboriginal groups and particular plants and creatures created in different regions of the country during the Dreamtime itself. It is expressly forbidden as part of the Law for any person to kill or eat the group's totemic animal, for this would be tantamount to violating the sacred bond with the Earth Mother. It is not unusual for an Aboriginal person to use the expression 'meat' or 'flesh' when they are referring to the totem animal that is sacred to their biological mother. Because she — and everyone else within the totemic group in turn has incarnated through the womb of a female Spirit Ancestor since the Beginning of the Dreaming — it is forbidden to kill or eat the totemic species that are linked with her.

Some Aboriginal groups differentiate totemic affiliations along basic gender lines so that there are Possum women and Kangaroo men, for example, and membership of these totemic groups is restricted on the basis of gender. Other groups recognise a two-fold division within their societies that anthropologists have referred to as 'moieties', from a Latin word meaning 'half'. Moieties can be matrilineal, meaning that children belong to the moiety of their mother, or they can be patrilineal, meaning that children belong to the moiety of their father. When a person marries, they are obliged to marry outside the moiety group. In the *Dua* and *Jiritja* moieties of Arnhem Land mentioned earlier, members of the former group must marry someone from the latter group. Often the moieties are identified by totems so, for example, the Brolga is the bird of the *Dua* moiety and the Jabiru is the bird of the *Jiritja* moiety, therefore Brolga people can only marry Jabiru people. Among the Gunditjmara people of Victoria, a *Kaputch* woman, symbolised by the black cockatoo, must marry a man from the *Krokitch* moiety, symbolised by the white cockatoo, and among many groups in south-eastern Australia an Eaglehawk man must marry a Crow woman, and vice versa. A universally observed principle applies here: that one does not partake of one's own totem — either in terms of killing and eating the totem species, or marrying within the group that is identified with it.

The women and men of the group will also have different totemic species that are uniquely assigned to them. Among the Wiradjuri, for example, a child of about ten years of age may be taken away from the main camp, by a native doctor who will 'sing' an assistant totem or *bala* into him. Healers and song-makers in all regions of the country will have spirit helpers to assist them with their ritual tasks, some of which may have first come to them in a dream.[2]

In some groups individual totems are linked primarily to an experience that heralds pregnancy. Just prior to a woman knowing that she is pregnant she, or her husband, may

Aboriginal boy, Clem Abbott, with magpie lark.

receive a sign that a spirit child has entered her womb — possibly in an unusual experience or in a dream. She may have a particular animal or bird cross her path which is a message that she is pregnant and consequently her child becomes spiritually linked to that being — which becomes an Ancestor and a particular Dreaming. Other groups link totems to where a child is born. In the Great Victoria Desert, for example, a man will endeavour to have his wife give birth to their children within his own 'country' — preferably close to a site or song line track associated with a totemic Ancestor. Among the Arrernte (or Aranda), on the other hand, where the child is conceived is more important than where the child is born. The right to own a sacred *tjurunga* (or *churinga*) — which literally embodies the vital force of the Spirit Ancestor — is determined by the 'conception site', and ownership of specific myths, ceremonies and chants is also decided on this basis.

In totemic awareness there is no division between the individual and the land, or between the Spirit Ancestor and individual custodians who both celebrate and incarnate the vital energy of that Ancestor. Neither is there any concept of the 'individual as creator' in traditional Aboriginal culture — all life and all creation emanates from the Ancestors. All Aboriginal descendants are the vehicles for ongoing creation and maintenance of the health and wellbeing of the land and its inhabitants. In ceremonies held to further the abundance of the totemic species, for example, the individual honours the dynamics of creation — reflecting with enthusiasm on what has been received in terms of sustenance from the land. Through performance of the ritual each person is participating directly in the sacred ceremonial cycles that help the Earth Mother and the Spirit Ancestors of the Dreamtime regenerate themselves upon the Earth.

FAMILY AND KIN

Kinship patterns provide the basis on which Aboriginal society is structured and this system of relationships is one which Aboriginal people maintain was established by the Dreamtime Ancestors — it has been like this since the Beginning of the Dreaming.

Aboriginal people are likely to have their closest relationships with their mother, their father, their grandmothers, their mother's brother, their father's sister and their cousins — these are the people who would be considered the most intimate members of the family. But an important principle operates in Aboriginal groups which makes the web of relationships easier to understand. Referred to by some as the 'classificatory' system of kinship, it basically means that siblings of the same sex are referred to by the same term and are regarded as being equivalent to each other. This means that two sisters are 'equivalent' to each other, as are two brothers. A child may call both his father and his father's brother by the same term, and in this way he or she has many 'fathers'. The child also has several 'mothers' and many brothers and sisters — for there is no special word for biological cousins in this system of terminology. A mother's brother is an 'uncle', a father's sister an 'aunt', and in some groups the same term is used for both grandparents and grandchildren. In talking to another related person most Aboriginal people would use terms like 'mother', 'auntie' or 'father', rather than calling the person by their individual name.

The classificatory system is also useful because it enables people who are meeting for the first time to work out how they should respond to each other in terms of 'proper relationship'. Because, somewhat like a kinship grid, the web of relationships reaches across the whole country. In the ultimate sense there are no strangers because potentially everyone is interconnected in one way or another. It is simply a matter of finding out how, for also inherent in the kinship system is obligations and reciprocity in relationships with others. John von Sturmer provides an interesting anecdote that relates how this is done:

> I recall travelling with an Aboriginal man, Mickey, from Edward River. We stopped at Mareeba to buy some food. Mickey remained in the vehicle. I observed an Aboriginal man walk past him along the footpath. He was clearly intrigued to find out who Mickey was, and Mickey was equally curious. The man walked backwards and forwards several times. Finally he came up to the vehicle and the conversation went something like this:

> *Mareeba man:* Where are you from?
> *Mickey:* I'm Edward River man. Where you from?
> *Mareeba man:* I'm Lama Lama man. . .do you know X?
> *Mickey:* No. Do you know Y?
> *Mareeba man:* No. Do you know Z?
> *Mickey:* Yes. She's my aunty.

Mareeba man: That old lady's my granny. I must call you daddy.

Mickey: I must call you boy. You give me a cigarette.[3]

When Aboriginal people across the country meet in this way — perhaps far from where they were born — they feel that they are part of an extended family and there is real joy and pride in this, for it is like a special bond. The practice of reciprocity in social relations was respected by all Aboriginal cultures and was underpinned by the understanding that those who did not give did not receive.

SKIN NAMES

According to tradition, many Aboriginal communities were divided by the Spirit Ancestors into what are now called 'skin names' or 'flesh' groups. People who belong to the same group are said to have the same 'skin' or flesh because they come from the same Spirit Ancestor. It is through knowing the skin or flesh name of a person that one can know her or his relationship to every other person within the larger community, as these skin or flesh group classifications cross over any localised tribal boundaries. Skin names also apply to other animal and plant species and to distinctive phenomena in their cosmology.

SKIN NAMES

Skin names provide a concise method to work out the social relationship — rights and obligations — between different individuals. It also directly relates to the people one may marry. In Central Australia, among the Warlpiri speakers, the men's names begin with J and women's with N. The following are the names that are used:

MALE	FEMALE
Jangala	Nangala
Jampijinpa	Nampijinpa
Jupurrula	Napurrula
Jakamarra	Nakamarra
Jungarrayi	Nungarrayi
Japaljarri	Napaljarri
Japanangka	Napanangka
Japangardi	Napangardi

The male skin names listed here are in father-son pairs. Thus Jangala's son will be called Jampijinpa and Japanangka's son will be called Japangardi. The first names in each pair belong to one generation level and the second (lower) names in each pair to another generation level. A person is obliged to marry someone who comes from their own generation level. The four pairs of skin names at the top of the list above represent one-half of Warlpiri society — described in anthropological literature as a 'moiety' — and the others lower down represent the other half. Individuals should marry outside their moiety. Ideal marriage partners would be as follows:

J / Nampijinpa	=	J / Napangardi
J / Nakamarra	=	J / Napaljarri
J / Napurrula	=	J / Napanangka
J / Nangala	=	J / Nungarrayi[4]

Above: *Muk-Muk* by artist Rover Thomas (Joolama), a Kukatja-Wangakajunga man, who lives at the Warmun community, Turkey Creek, Western Australia. Courtesy Kimberley Art.

When Aboriginal people come into another group's country they not only adopt a respectful attitude to the land of their hosts, but they also have to be brought into the kinship system of that group. The visitor is ascribed social status and an appropriate kin or skin name to enable them to operate within the new context. In addition, they also have to become acquainted with specific customs and social activities that relate to that particular territory and group of inhabitants.

KINSHIP AND SACRED TERRITORY

The relationship between Aboriginal culture and the land is further emphasised by the fact that their kinship structure is completely enmeshed and defined by the concept of sacred territory. All Aboriginal tribes occupy and own a distinct area of territory where they hunt and forage for food and observe rules and customs in relation to it. Indeed the very concept of a tribe — as distinct from a language group — is that it inhabits and 'owns' (or has custodianship for) a specific area of the country. The ceremonial rites related to the territory in each case will differ from the local customs observed by neighbouring groups, and in this sense there are distinct boundaries in relation to land. Often natural features in the landscape define the tribal boundaries because these landscape features may have acquired their significance during the Dreamtime. Dreamtime mythology bonds the tribal group to the land. As a rule Aboriginal people only feel really safe and secure when they are on their own clan lands.

As we have already seen, any given 'country' is the home of Spirit Ancestors and prominent landmarks are associated with these beings and with the Aboriginal descendants who belong to this 'country'. Implicit in a person belonging to a particular country, rather than the country belonging to a person, is specific custodial responsibilities in caring for this country. For these reasons alone a tribal group would not seek to take over the lands of another group because that would entail also taking over associated cycles of mythology, and secret information revealed only to initiates — which is forbidden. Such an invasion of another group's spirit home would be a heinous violation of the Dreaming — the Law. It goes without saying that the invasion of white settlers on Aboriginal territory has had a disastrous effect on the mythic links between Aboriginal peoples and their designated sacred lands.

As said earlier, a substantial mythic cycle may relate to several tribal countries, and different groups therefore 'own' different parts of the myth in a custodial sense. This means that each of the groups depends on each other in order to preserve the mythic cycle as a whole. Since the welfare of the tribes and their links with Nature are intimately connected with the Spirit Ancestors and their Dreamtime myths, vast holistic networks of relationship arise over very large areas of the landscape. These relationships are further reinforced by the practice of ceremonial rites.

SPIRIT HOMES

Overriding all of these mythic and ceremonial distinctions, however, is the important idea that each person belongs to the land by virtue of having been conceived and born there — it is really they who are owned by the land rather than the other way around. One cannot venture away from one's spiritual territory for too long without endangering one's life. One's own country is where all the spirit homes are; everyone who has been born upon the land is believed to have pre-existed in a spirit home at certain locations within the spirit country. A person is essentially linked to their land because it is where the true home of their spirit resides and because all the spirits of all the individuals who make up the local group come from spirit homes within the tribal territory. The spirit homes themselves were created by the Spirit Ancestors during the Dreamtime: individual human spirits were left at various locations as the Ancestors engaged in their travels across the land. This means that every Aboriginal person is linked to their family by something much more profound than pure kinship or genealogy in the western sense of the word. They are linked very specifically by a shared spiritual origin.

Opposite: *Arnkerrthe* [Mountain Devil Lizard] *Dreaming* by artist Gloria Temarre Petyarre, an Anmatyerre woman, who lives in the Utopia community in the Northern Territory.

THE ABORIGINAL IDEA OF THE FAMILY

Quite obviously, the Aboriginal concept of 'family' is clearly different from that which is found in contemporary white Australian culture, and elsewhere in the modern western world. In a traditional context, the Aboriginal family was always on the move within the context and confines of the sacred and totemically delineated 'country', always in transit from one campsite to another. And the composition of the family or 'band' could vary, because from time to time individual members married or died, while others transferred to or from other groups because of kinship or ceremonial obligations.

The number of people in the 'travelling band' could vary in size from a small individual family to a larger gathering of around 50 people. Typically a larger hunting and foraging group would include several older men, as well as women from different families who could hunt smaller animals and gather sufficient bush tucker to support not only themselves but also the young and elderly members of their group.

When mention is made of a traditional Aboriginal 'family' it usually means a group of people who sleep at the same campsite location and who help and support each other in everyday activities. However, in Aboriginal families there have always been distinctive female and male roles and also a clear gender-based demarcation in terms of who camped where and who married whom.

Especially among Aboriginal people living in the desert regions, and perhaps because of the relative scarcity of food in these areas, the social roles were distinct and so too were the camping procedures. In general terms traditional Aboriginal families seem to have opted for a pattern that has few features in common with western ideas of the 'nuclear family'. The structure of the extended family band apparently developed primarily as a response to the gathering of food, and divided itself along clear gender lines:

> In traditional times when the group was travelling from camp site to camp site it is likely, that the sexes walked more or less separately, each going about his or her own tasks in the food quest…At night a woman would share her day's collection with her immediate family while the men's hunting gains were cooked and shared with a wider circle…

> Perhaps then the Aborigines did not share our concept of the nuclear family as a residential and operational unit. This would explain the myths in which groups of men or groups of women are described as travelling independently. Groups consisting of sisters, or mothers and children, brothers, brothers-in-law, fathers and sons, or mothers' brothers and sisters' sons are seen as more logical units than man, wife and children.[5]

THE EXTENDED FAMILY

The immediate extended family is the most important social group for any Aboriginal person. Some Aboriginal family groups are matrilineal and others patrilineal. A matrilineal extended family might consist of one's mother and her husband, their children, the mother's mother and sisters, the sisters' husbands and the daughters' husbands. The men who had married into the family would, in this instance, be considered as the brothers of these women. A typical patrilineal extended family, on the other hand, might consist of one's father and his wife, their children, the father's brothers and father, and the son's sons,

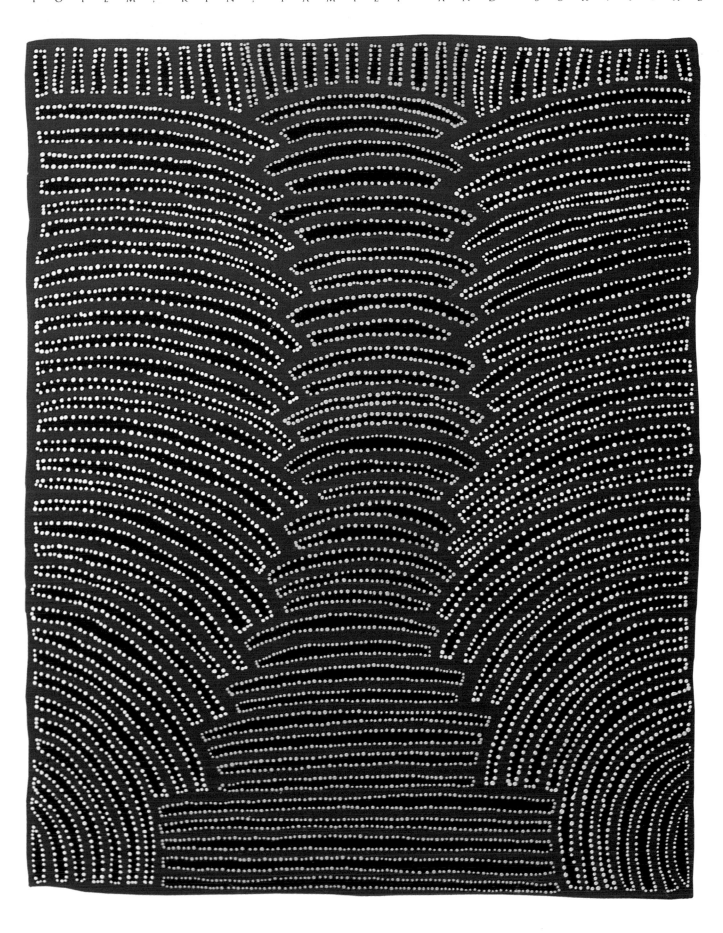

Totemic Ancestors of
Bopalinmar by Patric Mudjana
from Ramingining in central
Arnhem Land. Courtesy of Coo-ee
Aboriginal Art.

X-Ray Kangaroos and Mimi Spirits by Gunbalanya (Oenpelli) artist Robin Nganjmira of the Gunwinggu (or Kunwinjku) people. *Mimi* figures are slender, stick-like spirits who are said to inhabit the bush and rock crevices in Arnhem Land. They are reputably fine hunters and are also regarded as very artistic as they liked to paint their portraits in red ochre on the rocks. In these portraits the *Mimi* depict themselves in various pursuits such as dancing, spearing kangaroos and hunting. *Mimi* spirits are not regarded as Creator Beings but are said to have taught the ancestors of the present-day Gunwinggu the art of painting. Although *Mimi* spirits have an enchanting quality, they can be both benevolent and malevolent. Courtesy of Coo-ee Aboriginal Art.

with the women who have married into the family considered as the sisters of these men. The family group — sometimes laughingly referred to as 'us mob' or 'our mob' — really consists, on an individual basis, of those who have married into the group. This is the Aboriginal notion of 'family'. As we have mentioned, in Warlpiri society, for example, custodial land is either *kurdungurlu* — related to a particular place, country or Dreaming on the 'mother's side' — and is complementary to *kirda* — all those related to a particular place, country or Dreaming on the 'father's side'.[6] The concept of the totemic family, as mentioned in kinship relations, also extends to creatures and features in the natural world.

The family group has the hunting and food gathering rights to its land, or more specifically, to its spiritual 'country'. Each group has a ' head man' — usually the oldest initiated male member of the group, irrespective of whether kinship is defined matrilineally or patrilineally — and the head men of various groups in the tribe constitute a council of elders. The council will meet periodically to discuss matters of common interest and to make important decisions, when the various local groups come together, for example for shared ceremonies, or *corroborees*. Senior women also exercise important power and influence within the group, and will meet from time to time to settle important community matters and to hold *yawulyu* (or *awelye*) or 'women's business' — ceremony exclusively for women but which relates to the wellbeing of the community as a whole.

THE NEWLY MARRIED COUPLE

In contrast to notions of the western nuclear family, in traditional Aboriginal groups the demarcation of the sexes which is already recognised from childbirth consolidates very distinctively after marriage. A recently married couple, for example, would build a small dwelling and camp around a single fire, but things would then change once the first child was born. The mother would now sleep on one side of the fire with the young child, while the father slept on the other side by himself. As more children were born the two-fold division would become even more distinct with one part of the campsite and several fires allocated to the mother and her children, and another part of the campsite and a single fire allocated to the husband. This pattern would continue until female children reached puberty and male children were considered ready for circumcision and initiation. In terms of their actual sexual relationship, traditionally Aboriginal couples have engaged in lovemaking away from the campsite and usually during the day, because the night time is potentially hazardous and evil spirits lurk in the dark.

RESOURCES AND SURVIVAL

As we have seen, Aboriginal peoples have a complex and extraordinarily rich spiritual and social life, all of which is interwoven with the land. Because of this intimate connection to the land and all of its features, Aboriginal groups probably retain the most detailed knowledge of all the diverse regions on the Australian continent. In the environments in which they live, traditional knowledge of the land provides them with a strong sense of security and confidence because all facets of their existence are basically familiar — and this is crucial to their survival. Aboriginal people have had to know their country intimately. They have had to be aware of the food resources available

in different regions and seasonal variations in that food supply, and they had to know where to locate sources of water.

This is not to say that Aboriginal groups have faced a uniform challenge across the country — for the nature of the terrain and the available food resources vary greatly from place to place. Aboriginal groups who lived on the northern coast, for example, would gather different types of food in different seasons according to availability. At certain times of the year their main source of food might come from estuary fishing, gathering shellfish and crustaceans at low tide, and perhaps hunting migratory birds like magpie geese. At other times plant foods like yams would be the major feature of the diet. The richer coastal areas of Australia, with higher rainfalls and more diverse and reliable vegetation, have traditionally sustained much larger populations than the arid desert regions of Central Australia. Along the coast the range of available seafood is diverse and the rainforests provide a plentiful supply of plant food and game.

In the Central Desert areas, on the other hand, Aboriginal groups moving from campsite to campsite had to know exactly where each water source was located — and this knowledge

Above: *Hunting for Yams* by George Milpurrurru, a Ganalbingu man, who lives at Ramingining in central Arnhem Land. Courtesy of Coo-ee Aboriginal Art.

was acquired from first-hand observation of seasonal rainfall, and through a knowledge of evaporation and drainage patterns. Fortunately in the desert, even though large pools of water may be scarce, underground sources of water are reasonably plentiful — if one knows where to look. There are always areas where water can be found, even in times of extreme drought.

This type of information has been crucial to Aboriginal survival. Desert-dwellers knew that certain plants — and even various species of frogs — stored water and were an additional water source for this reason. Aboriginal women would often carry water in large *coolamons* — elongated wooden bowls — if they were venturing into desert regions where there was no readily accessible water, and some Aboriginal groups in Central Australia also used kangaroo skin bags to transport water in the desert. Interestingly, this practice did not extend into the very arid regions of the Western Desert because of religious taboos associated with kangaroos.

FOOD, FIRE AND RAIN

In times of drought the most pressing problem is not the scarcity of water so much as a lack of available food growing near the areas of permanent water supply. Paradoxically the areas of the desert with the poorest soils — areas where spinifex is found growing abundantly — are also the regions where the greatest amount of plant food can be found. Often groups of useful plant species grow near each other in areas close to a water supply.

Generally a desert forager might expect to be able to find plant food at most times of the year — except perhaps during the two coldest months, when plant growth was slow and some fruits and plants could be adversely affected by frost. Bush food is generally available in most seasons, although at certain times one would have to work harder to get it. The introduction by Europeans of rabbits and grazing animals like cattle, has also had a detrimental effect on traditional Aboriginal food-gathering practices because the largest concentration of these animals is in drought refuge areas — and they have taken food resources away from the native species.

Allocating increasing amounts of land to grazing animals has also had an adverse effect on Aboriginal land-burning practices — techniques of using controlled burning to enhance plant productivity. It has been estimated that of the twelve most important plants in the traditional Aboriginal economy, five are 'fire weeds' — plants that require regular burning if they are to attain their maximum production. Three of the others are fire tolerant, while the remaining four are intolerant to fire.[7] However, Aboriginal groups know how to control fire in their traditional environment: they know that certain plant species regenerate after controlled burning, and that in this way the production of various plants can be maximised. They also use fire to smoke out animals from hollow trees or to drive them out from dense vegetation into an ambush.

In situations where Aboriginal fire techniques are no longer practised, a dramatic shift in the balance of natural species can occur. It is known in Central Australia, for example, that a number of desert mammals were very prevalent prior to the establishment of Aboriginal settlements in the 1930s and 1940s, but by the time scientific studies were carried out in the 1970s species like the Burrowing Bettong, the Golden Bandicoot and the Desert Bandicoot had vanished, and the Rufous Hare-wallaby has now become virtually extinct — probably because of the change in the fire regime. It is also interesting to note that with the movement of Aboriginal people into settlements, wildfires — by definition, uncontrolled fires — returned to Central Australia. As Penny Van Oosterzee has written: 'Particularly after a wetter period, such as occurred in 1973–74, fires razed tracts of land the size of European countries: wildfires in the summer of 1974–75 burnt 120 million hectares [296 million acres] of land.'[8] It goes without saying that in traditional Aboriginal family life fire is used to cook the food and provides warmth and light in the camps at night. Fire also plays a central role in the ceremonial lives of Aboriginal peoples and is treated with great respect.

One of the most difficult times for gathering food is during the weeks which follow drought-breaking rain. At this time the larger native animals disperse and the plant foods in the region may often be spoiled. It is comparatively easier to track animals during times of drought because their distinctive markings are left on the bare ground and they can be more readily hunted around the few waterholes and scarce regions of green vegetation which exist.

It should also be emphasised that Aboriginal hunters are awesome trackers who notice details of animal movements that would go unnoticed by the untrained eye. Tracking is a learned science and also an art form which involves far more than just observing footprints

on the ground. It is a total observation of known patterns, and breaks in these patterns, developed over time into second nature and also a sixth sense which involves anticipation of what a certain species of animal is likely to do, given certain options.

FAMILY HUNTING IN THE DESERT

Central Australia is a region of harsh extremes and Aboriginal groups have had to adapt to the prevailing conditions in order to stay alive. As far as we know, prior to the arrival of European settlers in Central Australia, Aboriginal peoples from the desert regions — groups such as the Warlpiri, Alyawarra, Pintupi, Wangkajunga and Kukatja — lived for most of the year in small kin-based groups which would travel across vast areas of land in accordance with the seasons and the availability of water and food. Their travels were also influenced by ceremonial observances linked to different regions of the country.

Generally the family group divided their hunting and foraging roles along gender-based lines of responsibility. As Yuka Napanangka, a Kukatja woman, commented: 'Morning again, father go hunting. . .Mother go out separate from father and come back with big mob animals. . .'9 Women hunted and gathered bush tucker in groups, while men usually hunted alone or in pairs. Women hunted for small animals like lizards, goannas, frogs, birds, echidnas and perentie lizards, and were also responsible for gathering edible roots, eggs, seeds and berries, as well as collecting other resources like ochre, resin, bark, wax, honey and spinifex. The men generally pursued larger game like kangaroos, emus and bush turkeys. The actual act of finding food required considerable effort and would often involve walking long distances before returning to camp each night with the spoils of one's endeavours. Meanwhile very young children would stay behind with their grandparents while their parents were away gathering food: 'Morningtime, father one bin go hunting long way way. . . Mother and father sometime bin come back late from hunting. . .They bin go long way.'10

In the desert regions it would seem that most of the food, perhaps up to 80 per cent of it, would come through the activities of the women. Finding plant food and tracking down the smaller animals was comparatively more reliable and predictable. Catching the larger animals could not always be guaranteed.

A favourite food source of many Aboriginal groups is the witchetty grub. Usually gathered by the women, witchetty grubs are the larvae of a large grey moth, and the grubs are found in the roots of the witchetty bush (*Acacia kempeana*). The grubs, which are approximately the size of a human thumb, have a nutty taste and are a good source of dietary protein and fats. Available all year round, they are generally lighted roasted on coals before being eaten.

In addition to gathering witchetty grubs and a variety of wild fruits and vegetables the women also collected seeds. However, the seeds would often be mixed in with plant matter and particles of dirt and sand. To overcome this difficulty the women became experts in a skillful process called *yandying* which was used to separate the seeds from twigs, leaves, stones and sand in order to retain what was edible. The process involved carefully rotating the seeds in a *coolamon* to separate out particles of different densities.

As the major food providers within the family group, the women usually generally decided when to move from campsite to campsite on the basis of available food and water resources. As Lumu Nungurrayi, a Wankajunga woman, recalls: 'We moved to another rock

Opposite: Ted Egan Jangala, master tracker of the Warlpiri people, teaching his son Derek the ancient skills of tracking.

hole and made camp there. The men went hunting and the women went walkabout. . .We start going walkabout again and get berries and seeds. Put them in our *coolamons* and take them back to camp. . .'[11]

What one caught or gathered on the land, one also had the right and obligation to distribute. The main priority was to feed the members of the immediate family group. The women might choose to distribute some of their gathered food to close women relatives while the men would give some of their *kuka*, 'meat catch', to other men with whom they had a political alliance. A kangaroo, for example, would be cooked and partially accounted for before it was brought back to camp, and women would similarly eat and divide some of their food among their friends before it was brought back to camp. However, once food had come to the camp in the evening, it was the responsibility of the women to undertake a subsequent distribution — usually on the basis of marriage ties, ritual relations and friendship. Recalling the distribution of food to the family, Milyika Napaltjarri, a Kukatja woman, remembers: 'Mother bin bring back lot of goanna, rabbit and meow [cat]. We used to get happy when we bin see them coming.'[12] And Ngunytja Napanangka Mosquito, a member of the Wangkajunga group, recalls: 'Kids hungry and they want to know when goanna come. Mother go back and get the cooked ones to feed everyone. . .When mother give us goanna we happy. . .We rub our face with the goanna fat to make it shiny after we finish eating.'[13]

HEALING PLANTS

Quite apart from the use of edible seeds and plants, many Aboriginal groups in Central Australia used traditional plants as healing remedies. Ranging from small herbs to large trees, around a third of these plant remedies came from *Acacia* and *Eremophila* species. Most had poisonous or bitter principles, and several contained a high proportion of aromatic substances.

A majority of the plant medicines — perhaps as high as 70 per cent — were used as wash or ointment because Aboriginal people had no utensils for boiling water and therefore couldn't attack the germs of disease in this way. Some plant medicines were pounded into a paste and mixed with fat to make an ointment which was then applied directly to the body. The gum from *Eucalyptus opaca*, for example, was often rubbed onto burns, sores or wounds.

Sometimes Aboriginal people used the fumes from heated leaves to assist the healing process, and here certain species of *Eremophila*, *Acacia* and *Eucalyptus* were very useful. Babies were often 'smoked' for a few minutes in the fumes from such plants 'to make them strong', but the method for treating adults was a little more elaborate. When adults were sick, a pit would be dug, slightly larger than the patient, and a fire lit within. When the fire had died down to coals, branches from the plant would be strewn across the coals and the sick person would lie on this bed of leaves until the fumes had ceased. In so doing, the patient would inhale the fumes from the burning leaves and build up quite a sweat. This practice was apparently very successful as a means of restoring health.[14]

Aboriginal boy with long-necked turtle. Courtesy of Wildlight.

*The spirits of the country gave women's
ceremonies to the old woman* [a term of respect for
age to describe the headwoman]. *The woman sings,
then she gives that ceremony to the others, to
make it strong. The old woman is the boss, because
the spirits of the country have given her the
ceremony. So all the women get together and sing.*

*The old women sing the ceremonies if people are
sick, they sing to heal young girls, or children...
The old women are also holding their country as
they dance. The old women dance with that in
mind, they teach the younger women and give
them the knowledge, to their granddaughters, so
then all the grandmothers and granddaughters
continue the tradition.*[1]

Chapter Seven

WOMEN'S BUSINESS, MEN'S BUSINESS

In Aboriginal society, as we have seen, both women and men share a common Dreamtime heritage and also have their spiritual bonds with particular Spirit Ancestors. However, in addition to rituals and ceremonies in which they both celebrate aspects of this shared heritage, there are also rituals that are sacred, and exclusive, to women, and rituals that are sacred, and exclusive, to men.

In identifying Spirit Ancestors and their creative actions, feelings and behaviours, the Dreamtime not only specifies particular links to the land, but also provides prototypes for the activities of women and men in daily life — and these are reflected in the Law. The sacred ritual activities pertaining to Dreamtime Law are known as 'business', and accordingly there is Law that is considered 'women's business' and Law that is considered 'men's business'. The ceremonial grounds where women enact their sacred rituals are taboo to men and vice versa. With regard to women's rituals the men are 'uninitiated', and to the men the women are 'uninitiated', and each is thus excluded from the sacred ceremonies of the other. Prior to her recent passing, senior Law woman, educator and beloved elder of the Ngariyin peoples, Daisy Utemorrah, said that it is only after men have obtained the highest degrees of male initiation 'only then do they become eligible for initiation into Women's Law.' Similarly only the senior older women would be admitted to the secret men's rituals. Women and men alike have their own sacred knowledge of the country, their own symbolic designs, songs and emblems, and their own ritual objects and practices.

In addition to exclusive women's and men's rituals, the sacred inheritance of the Dreamtime — the *Tjukurrpa* or *Alcheringa* — also includes a number of fertility, mourning and increase ceremonies in which both women and men play their part. On these occasions the ritual demarcations within different ceremonial performances are clear and distinct. However, much of the sacred ritual and symbolism of the men — such as that utilised in the fertility rituals — imitates the physiological and reproductive processes of woman. So both female and male principles are represented, even in gender exclusive rites. Nevertheless, while certain ritual roles are enacted separately and are even taboo to the opposite gender, within the larger scheme of things all sacred ritual knowledge is undertaken for the benefit of the

Opposite: Women 'painting up' in ceremony at Yuelamu community, Mount Allen, Northern Territory.

whole community. If a healing ritual, for example, is performed by the women for a sick person, this is seen to benefit not only the individual but also the family and community of which that person is a member. At a very fundamental level, the philosophy which underscores traditional Aboriginal life is essentially one of cooperation and interdependence.

It needs to be emphasised, too, that rituals are not simply a matter of religious faith that may or may not be acted upon. Based on extensive knowledge, they involve considerable planning and protocol and require faithful and strict adherence to Dreamtime Law as delineated by the Ancestors. Many ceremonies extend for several days or weeks, even years, and to this extent they are rightly regarded as hard work.

LIVING APART

In traditional Aboriginal society women and men have separate camps and spend much of their time apart — in the activities of daily life there is a clear demarcation between their respective roles. Women usually spend the day in the company of other women and care for the children, while men socialise with other men. Even when a hunting party goes off in search of food it is likely that groups of women will forage for bush tucker and hunt smaller animals — teaching the children as they go — while the men go off separately in pursuit of larger game. In the evenings the men and women come together, the food is shared as are entertainments, such as story-telling and singing, and the day's activities together with important family concerns are discussed. In traditional life, this probably is the main period of the day when women and men spend time together. To a large extent the lives of women and men are independent and autonomous, but within the context of the family group and in terms of mutually caring for the welfare of their group and their cultural heritage they are interdependent. Both in daily life and in ritual life, women and men acknowledge their need and respect for each other — they are two parts of a symbiotic whole.

At the end of an evening's activities people again return to their separate camps. In the case of women in Central Australia, for example, their separate dwelling is known as the *jilimi* — the single women's camp — and it is from here that women's ritual activity largely emanates. The single women's camp, like the women's ceremonial ground, is an area that is taboo to men. It is considered a safe place and also a power base for women. Those who reside in the *jilimi* include the powerful and much respected senior Law women. These women are not only the repositories of sacred ritual knowledge and wisdom but they also wield major influence in the entire spectrum of Aboriginal cultural life in their communities. And culture in Aboriginal life, as we have said, includes everything. Also resident in the *jilimi* are the unmarried younger women, women perceived as too young or not yet ready to go to husbands, widows who have chosen not to remarry, women visitors and also women who may be 'married' but who for various reasons do not live with their husbands. In traditional life a *jilimi* would shelter only a few women; however, in settled communities each *jilimi* might have as many as two dozen residents, and as a campsite it is regarded as a potent symbol of female autonomy.

THE WORLD OF WOMEN

In most early documenting of Aboriginal cultures, the unique spiritual knowledge, skills and contributions of Aboriginal women to their societies were given scant attention by white

Women's ceremonial dancing at *corroboree*, Yuelamu community, Mount Allen, Northern Territory.

Katatjuta (the Olgas) in the
Northern Territory is an
important sacred site to the
Pitjantjatjara and the
Yankuntjatjara peoples — or
Anangu — and especially to the
Aboriginal women of these tribes.

observers, or neglected altogether. When the early anthropologists — most of them Anglo-European educated men — visited Aboriginal groups and endeavoured to document their cultural activities, the women were usually ignored, regarded as peripheral or at worst defined as the 'profane' members of society. These researchers assumed — as in their own cultures — that the men were more significant, and thus used the regional information they gained from Aboriginal male informants as being applicable to 'Aboriginal culture' as a whole.

Traditionally female custodians can speak of their sacred traditions only to women and male custodians only to men. Although men and women may be aware of each other's ritual and ceremonial lives, they neither have the authority to speak nor will they publicly acknowledge this knowledge. As Aboriginal women were rarely asked about their lives by white male researchers, very little information was elicited. Their place in Aboriginal life was relegated to that of the domestic — as providers of food, children and sex — in a culture thought to be dominated by men, and where women were of secondary importance. White scholars deemed that only Aboriginal men were the custodians of the 'sacred' traditions. The complementary nature of Aboriginal women's and men's contributions to both sacred and mundane aspects of their cultures was unknown in the written record. That Aboriginal women and men shared the sacred trust of the Dreamtime, that their respective roles were acknowledged, respected and seen as integral to the welfare of the life and traditions of their cultures was not officially recognised in the academic world until 1939 when anthropologist Phyllis Kaberry published the findings of her work with Aboriginal women.[2] Kaberry's work evidenced that Aboriginal women are full participants in their societies with their own sacred and powerful ritual traditions in which they have, within the context of their traditional responsibilities, total independence and full autonomy.

Further support for this evidence has come with the findings of other women researchers such as Catherine Berndt, Jane Goodale, Isobel White, Diane Bell and others.[3] All of these women lived and worked with Aboriginal women, in different communities throughout the country, who could relay their own cultural knowledge.

It is now clear that almost all earlier research, despite containing some valuable knowledge on traditional Aboriginal life, is inaccurate with regard to Aboriginal women and presents a distorted view of what actually occurs in Aboriginal societies. It is only since the 1970s that a more balanced perspective has begun to emerge.

Aside from the issue of documentation on Aboriginal cultures, there is now an increasing awareness of Dreamtime myths, from different regions throughout the country, which relate how originally it was the ancestral women, rather than the male heroes, who were the holders of many of the most sacred rituals and objects within the culture. The Djan'kawu Sisters mythical song line which underpins the most important rituals of the *Dua* moiety of Arnhem Land — the *dua nara* — shows how the women's songs, rituals and the sacred emblems in their dilly bags were stolen from them by the men they had created. As we mentioned earlier, the men took control of not only the women's songs and sacred objects but the power of the sacred ritual which had previously belonged solely to the women. In the fertility rituals of the Djan'kawu, the most attention is given to this section of the myth. It is said in the myth that the women relinquished the power of these rituals to the custodial care of the men with the knowledge that they themselves remained sacred and, besides which, they already knew everything about the sacred material. They also recognised that they had their wombs which were the real source of creative power and not just its symbolic representation. Imagery from the extraordinary Djan'kawu mythology is seen in the work of well-known bark painters and elders of the Yolngu, the late Wandjuk Marika and Mathaman Marika, and in the linocut work of artist Banduk Marika — all of the Yirrkala community in Arnhem Land.

Arrernte myths from Central Australia also affirm that the female Spirit Ancestors celebrated in their myths were 'dignified and sometimes awe-inspiring figures, who enjoyed unlimited freedom of decision and action. Frequently they were much more powerful beings than their male associates. . .'[4] They also relate how women owned the sacred emblems and played roles equal to that of the men. Similarly, most myths of the Great Victoria Desert imply that women originally possessed all the sacred rituals and emblems. They tell how women first circumcised such beings as Njirana, and how the Galaia or Emu Women taught the men how to use a stone flake instead of a fire-stick as the circumcision implement because many of the men's novices had died. In the Western Desert south of Wirrimanu (Balgo Hills), women in the Dreamtime era are said to have possessed all the sacred rituals but later had them taken away by the men, while in western Arnhem Land the *ubar* rituals belonged solely to the women until Gandagi, a Kangaroo Man, took the sacred emblems and ritual dances from the headwoman

Mingau, a Kangaroo Woman of the Fire Dreaming. Gandagi then assembled the men and they performed this ritual. This is how women lost control of the fire that originally belonged to them. A version of this myth tells how Gandagi had difficulty getting the dance steps right until he was shown how to do them properly by the women.[5] Similarly the Arnhem Land *kunapipi* rituals are said to have once belonged to the women. Such myths can be interpreted in a number of ways, but they do explain to some degree the relationships that exist between women and men and how they came to be.

In addition to the widespread mythical testimony that women's sacred knowledge existed prior to the knowledge belonging to the men, from what is now known about Aboriginal women's lives there can be no question that these women have retained their sacred knowledge and continue to perform their own rituals. In so doing they make contributions which are vital to Aboriginal spiritual life and survival, as they have done since the dawn of time.

Since the 1970s, and increasingly through the 1980s and 1990s, Aboriginal women from different communities are concerned to preserve their culture for future generations and are speaking out about their traditional knowledge. They are also sharing with outsiders some of their ceremonial life based on Dreamtime Law, such as aspects of their *yawulyu* (or *awelye*) their land-based ceremonies. In 1993, for example, sixteen senior Law women from the Wirrimanu (Balgo Hills) community in the Tanami Desert of Western Australia came to Sydney, accompanied by their exuberant paintings, and invited interested women to join them in an experience of their *awelye* in an effort to convey the rich spiritual legacy of their Dreamtime traditions. Author Anna Voigt was invited to attend and, along with other women, participated in part of the Tjipari song cycle. This involved being 'painted-up' with appropriate symbolic body designs followed by joining a ritual dance sequence — led by the senior custodians of this Dreaming — of Ancestral Women as they moved through the land creating, gathering and preparing food. From the beginning to the end of this 'little ritual' the Aboriginal women sang the Ancestral songs. All the non-Aboriginal women who took part in this rite were profoundly moved by the experience and by the knowledge, nurturance and generosity extended to them by the Aboriginal women.

Every Aboriginal woman has her own Dreamings, and by definition these are her custodial responsibility. A woman may be aware of the content and ritual activities associated with other Dreamings, but may only speak of her own. In a traditional context, Aboriginal women's rituals are often elaborate and may last for several days:

> Women's 'business' is usually performed away from the main living area, at a site out of ear-shot from it. It is often in an important food-gathering area and the women arrive at the ceremonial ground with food which they have collected along the way. Once on the ceremonial ground, they divide into two contiguous groups sitting in a semi-circle around a fire lit in the middle of a cleared area. They commence singing and beating their thighs in a metronomic pulse, with the most senior woman, the song owner, leading the performance. After some preliminary singing and dancing, some of the women from the side of the song leader go away to an obscured area at some distance from the singers and paint their bodies. Both the singers and the dancers must sing during the painting of the body designs. When these are completed, the two

dancers involved in the next item in the song series move towards the dancing area with their designs covered. As the song leader commences the appropriate song the dancers reveal their body designs simultaneously with commencing to dance towards the singing group. Whenever the singers pause for a break the dancers turn their backs to again obscure the design, turning when the singing recommences; and when they finally reach the singers, who then stop singing, they obliterate the design from their bodies. Senior women come forward and touch the dancers to earth the great power that has been released through them during their performance.

A women's ceremony may last for up to five days, with the women returning home each evening and coming back to the ceremonial ground each morning. The songs depict the journey of a particular Ancestor through the singer's country, and each item, of about 30 seconds duration (which is repeated many times) describes one place or event along the route. Dancing songs last longer than descriptive songs (perhaps up to four minutes with pauses within this time). The whole ceremony moves through the song series gradually, with many repetitions and pauses for informal chatter and laughter. The song leader, any time she feels that the group is losing concentration, reiterates the present song. In this way, a song needed for a particular body design, for instance, can be kept active over a period of one or two hours if necessary.[6]

When a woman expresses a Dreaming through a sacred ritual performance she is infused by and embodies the vitality of her Spirit Ancestors, affirms the deep and eternal bond with the land and is thus spiritually empowered within the context of the Dreamtime mythology.

For the most part women's rituals focus on their role as nurturers of the land and sustainers of the family and community's health, wellbeing and relationships, in preserving the Dreamtime heritage. As we have said, among the most important women's rituals are the *yawulyu* (or *awelye*), and the *yilpinji* (sometimes referred to as *jarada* or *djarada* in parts of South Australia). The *yawulyu* (or *awelye*) — that is, women's land-based ceremonies — and their love rituals, or *yilpinji* (or *ilbindji*), which as Diane Bell[7] has observed, are concerned with the 'emotional management' of the whole of Aboriginal society.

YAWULYU AND AWELYE

These terms are used extensively by women in Central Australia and Western Australia respectively to refer to their land-based rituals and ceremonies. *Yawulyu*, or *awelye*, is a broad-based term used to describe the sweep of attachments and responsibilities to country and the rituals that accompany them. Women's *yawulyu* rituals seek to reaffirm those traditional connections between their Spirit Ancestors and the land, which have existed since time immemorial. They also refer to rituals directed towards maintaining the health and harmony of both the land and human relationships, and are used to help resolve any conflicts and tensions in the community. As 'nurturing' rituals in the wider sense, *yawulyu* and *awelye* restore health, wellbeing, love and harmony within the context of the women's sacred *Tjukurrpa* heritage. Women's *yawulyu — or awelye —* and their love rituals, or *yilpinji*, are all underwritten by the Dreamtime legacy that is the Law which lives on through present generations of Aboriginal peoples. Aboriginal women in honouring

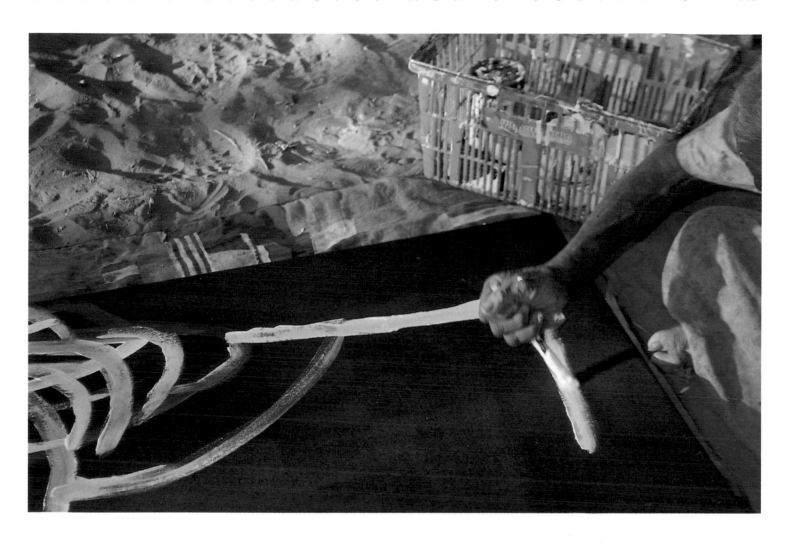

their Ancestors and singing the health of the land and the people consider that they 'grow up the country' and also 'grow up kin'.

Something which is common to all *yawulyu* ceremonies is the celebration of the women's sacred 'country' based on the custodial rights and responsibilities of those who are taking part. A woman's right to participate in *yawulyu* or *awelye* rituals is based on her responsibilities for specific areas of land associated with both her mother's and father's people. Through rights of descent traced through each of her parents, a woman has two different 'countries'. She is the 'owner' (*kirda*) of her father's country and the 'manager' (*kurdungurlu*) of her mother's country, and it is this dual responsibility which binds both men and women together in a sacred association with family land.[8] A woman also enjoys a special relationship to what is called one's *jaja* (granny) country from one's mother's mother. However, the *yawulyu* rituals themselves are performed as 'closed ceremonies' away from the men. Women have their own camps, and their own 'ring place' — their sacred ceremonial area — both of which, as we have said, are taboo to men.

The visual symbols used in the *yawulyu/awelye* have been dramatically expressed in the paintings of well-known Utopia community artists and Anmatyerre Law women, the late

The eminent artist, the late Emily Kame Kngwarreye, an Anmatyerre woman from the Northern Territory.

Above: *Awelye* (women's business) by artist Gloria Temarre Petyarre, an Anmatyerre woman, who lives in the Utopia community in the Northern Territory. Courtesy of Utopia Art.

Emily Kame Kngwarreye and sisters Gloria Temarre Petyarre and Kathleen Petyarre. Kathleen describes the *awelye* in her community, north-east of Alice Springs:

The old women used to [and still do] paint the ceremonial designs on their breasts, first with their fingers, and on their chests, and then with a brush called a *typale,* made from a stick. They painted their thighs with white paint. They painted with red and white ochres. Then they danced, showing their legs. The old women danced with a ceremonial stick and a headdress of feathers. While they danced they placed the ceremonial stick in the earth.

The spirits of the country gave women's ceremonies to the old woman [a term of respect for age to describe the headwoman]. The woman sings, then she gives that ceremony to the others, to make it strong. The old woman is the boss, because the spirits of the country have given her the ceremony. So all the women get together and sing.

The old women sing the ceremonies if people are sick, they sing to heal young girls, or children. If a child is sick in the stomach, they sing. The old women are also holding their country as they dance. The old women dance with that in mind, they teach the younger women and give them the knowledge, to their granddaughters, so then all the grandmothers and granddaughters continue the tradition.[9]

In talking generally about the *awelye* in her well-known paintings, Gloria Temarre Petyarre says: '*Awelye* proper body paint for my country. . .proper one for women looking after country. *Awelye* might be whole mob of women. . .might be body paint. . .might be little hills. . .might be little rainbows. . .'[10] Underpinning all of Gloria's work is her consciousness of her sacred traditional responsibilities. When Gloria paints, she — like other Aboriginal artists — sings the relevant Dreaming. In this way, Aboriginal artists are retracing the travels of their Ancestors in the mind's eye and this then unfolds as part of the creative act, yielding its imagery upon the canvas or bark surface of the artwork.

Jenny Green, who worked in the adult education program at the Utopia community, described her initial acquaintance with the women of Utopia, and the ceremonies which form the basis of their lives and artwork:

The country was revealed to me through the performance of elaborate song cycles and dances. Every afternoon the women congregated and prepared for the *awelye*. They smeared their bodies with animal [goanna] fat and traced the ceremonial designs on their breasts, arms and thighs, using brushes called *typale* (made from flat sticks with cotton). These were dipped in powders ground from charcoal, ash, and red and yellow ochre. The paintwork was appraised critically by everyone and mistakes or omissions of detail corrected. The women sang as each took her turn to be 'painted up'.

The singing continued for hours, interspersed with dance. Several women who had been appointed danced together, led on many occasions by Emily [Emily Kame Kngwarreye], the most senior woman of the Alhalkere clan. She carried the ceremonial painted stick (*kwetere*). Meanwhile the other women beat the rhythm with their hands, and sang the songs relevant to the Dreaming story. These depict the travels of the Dreamtime Ancestors through Alhalkere country, including the mountain devil lizard (*arnkerrthe*), the emu (*arnkerre*) and the kangaroo (*aherre*) and other totemic plants, animals and natural forces.[11]

In July 1991, Diane Bell recorded and participated in a *jarada*, a closed women's ceremony held at Nutwood Downs in the Roper River area which women from communities far and wide attended.

In song and dance, in gesture and design, the assembled women celebrated the travels of the Munga Munga Ancestral Women who pioneered the country from

Tennant Creek to Arnhem Land. They scattered across the Barkly Tablelands; they travelled from Macarthur River and from the junction of the Wilton and Roper Rivers to a site on Hodgson River and thence to Nutwood Downs, where their tracks divide, one following the 'road' to Alice Springs, the other to a site on Brunette Downs. The Munga Munga assumed different forms, met with, crossed over, absorbed and transformed the essence of other Ancestors; their influence infused country with the spiritual essence of women.[12]

In the *jarada* ceremony the assembled Aboriginal women retraced in song and dance the extensive travels of the Munga Munga Women. In this way they provided a graphic representation of the links forged between groups in the Dreamtime. Within the context of this overarching responsibility for the Dreaming, women also stated their responsibility for particular tracts of land and emphasised certain themes — as with Central Australian women, emotional management and health were the principal ones.

At one level women gave form to a generalised notion of their responsibility for land, its Dreamings and sites, in expressions such as 'we must hold up that country', 'not lose him, hold him tight' — such as that expressed earlier by Matingali Bridget Matjital — but at another level the ceremony allowed a certain division of labour for responsibility for country to be played out. In the dancing the women marked out the extent of the country of each language group.

Bell explains that because of the closed nature of the ceremony she cannot publicise details, however: '. . .in the Munga Munga ceremony women demonstrated their rights and responsibilities in land in both a generalised and particularistic fashion.' In their ritual lives Aboriginal women are independent, autonomous ritual actors who actively participate in the creation, transmission and maintenance of the values of their society.

Men were rigidly excluded from the Munga Munga ceremony, but at the conclusion of the activity on the ceremonial ground the women entered the main camp 'where the men had been sitting quietly. A gift exchange between men and women then took place. In this way the interdependence of men's and women's worlds was celebrated.'[13]

YILPINJI

The aspect of *yawulyu* related to Aboriginal women's 'emotional management' rituals is broadly referred to as *yilpinji. Yilpinji,* like all rituals, are underpinned by Dreamtime myths and their connections to land and the activities of the Ancestors — who also reflected emotional behaviour. The rituals are also greatly respected by the men as well as by the women, as both understand their power and relevance.[14] As mentioned earlier, this Central Australian term has been roughly and narrowly translated as 'love magic' and is described in terms of being primarily concerned with individual sexual matters, such as attracting a desired lover. However, Diane Bell, who embarked on a detailed field study of these rituals, learned that the concerns expressed in the powerful *yilpinji* rituals are much wider. They are in fact concerned with the entire spectrum of female and male relationships and the maintenance of harmonious relations in the whole of Aboriginal society.

Although on occasions a *yilpinji* ritual may be directed towards attracting a desirable marriage partner, this is undertaken in terms of 'right skin' and socially sanctioned relationships. Though even in these cases, the rituals have broader ramifications. Women and men come together in marriage and both may be inclined to perform love rituals beforehand with their own intent in mind. Nevertheless, whether it is a matter of 'women's business' or 'men's business' the 'love magic' rituals still have to do with the welfare of the group as a whole, because the bond of marriage itself occurs within the dictates of the Law, and the marriage of two individuals has implications for a much wider group of people.

Yilpinji songs and ceremonies honour and celebrate the power of emotions and feelings within the whole community. The highly charged and potentially volatile nature of emotions and feelings between the sexes is well understood in Aboriginal life. Feelings are also understood to be integral in spiritual communication and human functioning and have important consideration in all aspects of life — the comment 'that is my feeling' will be understood, respected and accommodated. As the actions of the Ancestors were encoded in their songs, so were their emotions, feelings and all manner of behaviours in response to these inner promptings — which are not without humour. Doing as the Ancestors did is the behavioural guide for their Aboriginal descendants, for emotions and feelings are seen to be powerful influences on behaviour. *Yilpinji* are the ritualised means whereby the imperatives of emotional expressions are given form and direction and thus serve to maintain stability within a community.

Yilpinji are performed by the 'owners' and 'managers' for particular Dreamings or country. Most of the *yilpinji* songs, designs and ritual enactments of the Warribri Kaytej (or Kaititj) women of Central Australia, for example, derive from the Dreamtime journeys of Ngapa (Rain Dreaming) and the Kurinpi (Old Women Dreaming) and also the travels of the Yawikiyi (Bush Berry Dreaming). In these *yawulyu* and *yilpinji* rituals, the central and intertwining themes of land, love and health are celebrated within the context of their Wakulpu and neighbouring countries. The authority of the Kaytej women is known with some degree of awe and they are called the 'Karlukarku women'. Karlukarlu is the name for the rock formation at Devil's Marbles near Wauchope and is also one of the names by which Aboriginal people refer to the surrounding country. Several of the major Dreamings which are held and celebrated by these women focus on Karlukarlu country and on Wakulpu, a site which gives its name to country further to the west. The areas contain much Ancestral activity. The behaviour in the myth which relates to *yilpinji* only occurs in the Devil's Marbles area because, say the Kaytej women: 'Our Dreaming for that area also has rainbow' — which refers to the Rainbow Men in the Dreaming story.[15]

The themes of land, health and love are embedded in the rituals in the central symbols of fat — goanna, emu or witchetty fat — and in certain colours, with their physical, emotional and spiritual associations. Colour and its powers of attraction is a major symbol of *yilpinji*. From the red of Karlukarlu rises the power of life force and blood. That power can be activated by women through massage with fat prepared during a performance of *yawulyu* for the country around Karlukarlu. This redness is counterpoised against the whiteness of rain and lightning flashing threateningly overhead at Devil's Marbles. This whiteness is disrupted and challenged by the brilliant display of the colours of the Rainbow Men who pursue women in the area — which is the focus of many of the *yilpinji*.[16]

All that is the colour black in Nature is associated with the Ancestral Being Yawakiyi

(Bush Berry). In his travels Yawakiyi faces bushfire, crosses over another Dreaming track and travels with Wardingi (witchetty). Yawakiyi is accompanied by his faithful bird companions, the Yirrpatirlpatirla (little black birds) and his life is dependent on Ngapa (water). He goes into the ground at Wakulpu (which is the boundary of responsibility of the Kaytej) to re-emerge further on, but the Kaytej women say 'Stop here. Don't run into someone else's country.'[17] The journeys of Yawakiyi depict correct ritual relations between *kurdungurlu* (managers) and *kirda* (owners) of country, mourning and the devotion of his bird friends who helped him survive his arduous journey.

In the *yilpinji* rituals of the Kaytej women underpinned by the Ngapa (Rain Dreaming) and Kurinpi (Old Women) myths, the brilliantly coloured and ever-changing Rainbow Men are referred to frequently. They can overpower women with their colour, wound them and thus draw women away from their land.[18] In one sequence in the Ngapa myth Ancestral Women have their sacred ritual objects — which hold the title deeds to country — stolen by men. The Ancestral Women, like most Dreamtime Women, usually carried their sacred ritual objects with them but decided one day to leave them behind in a tree while they went hunting with two men they had recently met. They returned to find their ritual packages missing, and when the women were reluctant to go with the two men the men speared them. (In both the *Kurinpi* and the rainbow myths the men beautified themselves to woo the women after they had wounded them.) In an Arrernte men's song cycle recorded by Strehlow,[19] the sequence of attraction, violence, consummation and travel to a new country is followed, and in Nancy Munn's account of Warlpiri male *yangaridji*[20] — which is closely related to *yilpinji* — the crippling is said to ensure fidelity. Finally, along with their mother, the Women went to the country of the men. In this myth, women's power — in the form of her sacred ritual paraphernalia — is stolen. Her ownership of country is weakened through this symbolic severance of her tie to the land.

In both rain (Ngapa) and bush berry (Yawiki) Dreamings, fat is the medium through which the power of the Dreaming is transformed and transmitted by the women who are *kirda* and *kurdungulu* for the country and the ceremonies. Fat is the central symbol of women's ritual in that it binds the principal themes of love, health and land. During the Spirit Ancestors creation journeys through the country, they rubbed themselves with fat and admired the redness and beauty of their bodies. To glow with health — and thus be attractive — is to be as the Ancestor covered with fat. Such obvious bodily health reflects contentment of being and the strength that comes to someone who has access to their Dreaming country.

The actual content of the *yilpinji* ceremonies remains sacred and secret, and is not revealed to women outside the ritual group. However, within the envelope of country, the myth-rituals include a rich blend of song, myth, dance and sacred body painting which includes that essentially female symbol, the circle. The vitality, beauty and creativity of these integrated oral, physical and spiritual rituals is difficult, if not impossible, to capture in the written form. As Diane Bell has commented: 'Certain *yilpinji* and health/curing designs are the same, because, as Kaytej women recognise, love, health and sexual satisfaction are intertwined at the personal and community level.' She continues, 'Exclusively, *yilpinji* designs concern agitation, excitement and longing. Such feelings are said to be located in the stomach that quivers and shakes like the dancing thighs of women, or the shaking leaves of men's poles at initiation, or the shimmering of a mirage, or the iridescence of a rainbow.'[21] After each performance all trace of the ceremonial activity on the ground is obliterated to void the *yilpinji* power and the ritual objects used in the ceremonies are then kept in a safe place under female supervision.

Women see both their own and men's colours as not static in a colour spectrum, but as ever-changing and as dramatic as the country itself — as mercurial and unpredictable as outcomes of female–male encounters and negotiations. The dynamics of respective gender values is given symbolic and metaphorical expression in ritual imagery. In both female and male versions of *yilpinji* myths there is the portrayal of love as crippling and the connection to the land as a living resource.

In *yilpinji* rituals women outline their prototypes of social reality and attempt to sculpt their worlds. They remember that certain actions and songs or complexes of songs were sung at a particular location for a specified person and gained a particular outcome. The ownership of myths and the custodial right to perform rituals gives women the power base for their claims to country, while the content of the myths explores women's independence and the composite nature of male and female encounters. The Ancestral Women in the myth embody, amongst other things, two conflicting principles in a woman's identity: on one level there is the need to be independent, while on another level there is the desire to have children, companionship and social exchange. The latter involves men, but simultaneously brings the challenge to women's autonomy and independence. It also brings the fear of men's unpredictability caused by their underlying insecurities. The myth explains male violence but without its justification. It serves rather to warn women of the treatment they may expect from men and of the potential dangers they face when leaving their own Dreaming country.

In all these ways and more is land, love and health symbolically and actually intertwined at every level. Land, country and sacred sites are aspects of a complex and detailed metaphysical knowledge system which bears no resemblance to Anglo-European systems and can only be touched through imaginal shifts in perception. To be understood the powerful *yilpinji* rituals need to be seen within the context of the land and the myths which underwrite them, and as a means of achieving socially sanctioned ends.

Karlukarlu (in the Devil's Marbles area) and Wakulpu are areas rich in Dreaming tracks and sites. Several of the major Dreamings which are held and celebrated by the Kaytej women focus on Karlukarlu country and on Wakulpu, and it is vital to the lives of these Aboriginal people that their rituals are performed there. However, when the main road from Alice Springs to Darwin was constructed it passed directly through the Devil's Marbles area and this has had a direct bearing on the ceremonial activities of the Kaytej people who live nearby. Some Kaytej women have said that they can still hear the old people crying from the caves because some of the most important rituals can no longer be performed there.

THE WORLD OF MEN

We have already mentioned the major transition which occurs when boys reach puberty: they undergo their first initiation which transforms them officially into men. Although circumcision is not universally practiced and other ritual procedures — like knocking out

Wardaman initiation rock at Ingeladdi, west of Katherine, Northern Territory.

teeth, extracting sections of skin or hair from the body, or making ritual cut-marks in the skin — may replace it, circumcision is nevertheless very widespread. More often than not circumcision is the major physical ordeal which boys undergo in their first initiation.

Among the Yolngu people of north-east Arnhem Land, for example, circumcision takes place over two weekends during the dry season and is considered the entry point for every Yolngu man in his quest for secret religious knowledge. As we said earlier, it is generally true

that women feature in certain sections of male initiation
ceremonies, although not those parts that are considered
secret or sacred for men. This is true of the Yolngu too, for
here the male rites of passage involve women in supportive
roles but not in the act of circumcision itself. The following
description of a male circumcision ceremony comes from
Ian Keen, who lived with the Yolngu during the late 1970s:

> The Honeybee ceremony was similar in form on all
> four days. On each day of the ceremony, men
> performed Honeybee and Spider-group songs,
> seated in a small group on blankets under the
> tamarind trees in Wurrpan's camp near the beach
> [Wurrpan was the leader of the group — a man in
> his seventies]. Other men who sat with the singers
> painted the initiands with red ochre and attached
> *Yirritja* moiety *wana* cords, of possum fur on a hair
> string base, to their arm bracelets. On all days but
> the first, the men danced with the boys to the
> cutting place, the 'place of blood', simply a
> designated area of the clearing where the women
> later prepared a hay mattress for the circumcision
> operation, some fifty metres from where they made
> preparations. On the final day three men
> circumcised the boys.[22]

Keen mentions that the songs, dances and body painting
increased in elaboration from day to day. The songs sung
included Freshwater and Inland Saltwater songs of the
Hollow Log ceremony — including Eel-tailed Catfish, Wild
Plum and Red Goshawk songs — and Forest songs,
including the Sulphur-crested Cockatoo, Cyclone, and
Emu. While the Forest songs were being performed,
women and girls also danced at the edge of the area,
lifting their feet to the clapstick rhythms and gesturing
responsively with their arms and hands — although they
kept well clear of the 'place of blood' where the
circumcisions were performed. On the final day the
ceremony was marked with Swamp songs, Forest songs, Frog and Fire songs, leading up
to a Fire Dance.

Fire rituals of one form or another are virtually universal across Aboriginal Australia as
part of the initiation process. Sometimes the young initiates are lowered by the older men
onto smoky fires or perhaps coals will be thrown at them. Then they may be obliged to join
the older men and trample the fires out with their feet. The fire ceremony certainly causes
pain, and to that extent is considered an ordeal — but it is also a source of ritual purification

and makes it 'safe' for the candidate to later return to the everyday world. Finally each candidate will bathe in water to wash away the embers from the fire, and in doing this he is symbolically 'washing away the sacred world' before returning to the main camp. There are usually special women's ceremonies to welcome back the young initiated men, for they have just undergone the most dramatic transformation of their lives so far and need the emotional support on their return.

There is no doubt that initiations like this leave a profound impact on the young men, for they have just experienced a major transition — a passage from one condition to another, which at times must seem almost like a journey through death itself. The intent of the initiation is to strengthen each candidate so that he may now be considered worthy to become a custodian of the male group's sacred mythology and ritual. And there is an emotional effect too:

> The contemplation of the heroes and ancestors of the past through the chanting of the myths and the handling of their sacred symbols, the frequent self-infliction of bodily pain, the dancing and the tense atmosphere in which the main acts occur, all work on the emotions, and at the same time cause all present to feel themselves as one.[23]

Sometimes there are different stages or degrees of a male initiation and during this cycle the candidate may be referred to by a general term rather than by his individual name. The following terms come from the Broome–Sunday Island district:

> *Leminem* is the candidate for tooth-knocking and he is so called during the rituals which are performed for a week preceding this operation. He is then a *Lainyar* until circumcision has been performed, usually a couple of days later; this makes him a *Palil* and a few secrets are revealed to him. Later on he is taken through an important blood ceremony, during which he is called *Djurdu* and at the end of which he is *Djaminanga* and is fitted to receive more advanced revelations. Some weeks or months later he is regarded as fit to give arm-blood for ceremonial purposes; his arms are ligatured, the blood taken and drunk, and he is now a *Gambel*; on a later occasion a wing of a bird is put in his head band and he is called *Rungor*; when the pearl shell public pendant is hung on him he is *Bungin*, and finally when he is admitted to the ranks of married men, he is ceremonially painted and known as *Mambangan*. He is now a man.[24]

Usually each young man receives a new individual name during his initiation — perhaps it is the name of a great Spirit Ancestor from the Dreamtime or the name of some other cultural hero. This name is considered so sacred that it would never be mentioned, except in hushed tones within the precincts of the sacred ceremonial ground. Sometimes, too, after the initiation, the young man may be given a special object, like a small piece of quartz, which becomes a personal symbol of the ritual transformation which has occurred. Such an object is highly valued because it embodies sacred qualities transmitted by the Spirit Ancestor — and it is always kept in a safe place.

Following the initiation the young initiate will also be shown sacred objects venerated by the other senior initiated men as part of the sacred heritage of the group. These might include wooden bullroarers associated with sky heroes or totemic beings, and *tjurungas*, which embody the vitality of Spirit Ancestors from the eternal Dreamtime. Because these objects are a source of sacred power, young initiates are awed by the opportunity to see and touch them for the first time — for here is a tangible connection with the Spirit Ancestors of the Creation Epoch. The sacred bullroarers and *tjurungas* are not retained by the young initiates, however, but are stored in special sacred storehouses watched over by the senior Law men of the group. Uninitiated people are not allowed to venture near these special storehouses, since they remain the exclusive domain of the initiated men within the group. The male *tjurungas* are only revealed on special occasions — at special men's ceremonies like initiations, at times when sacred power is needed to restore health to a sick man, or as a talisman taken on the hunt to ensure success. In this last instance, food gained through such means is considered sacred and may only be eaten by those who have been initiated.

It should perhaps be emphasised, too, that although the first major male initiation is the one whereby a boy becomes a man, certain men may be given different initiations throughout their lives and these initiations relate to specific custodial and ceremonial obligations. Without these additional initiations, for example, a man would not obtain privileged information about certain Dreaming sites, or acquire the knowledge required to become a senior Law man.

RITUAL OBLIGATIONS

As we have said, once a man has been initiated he has clear obligations, as a custodian of specific sacred lands and totemic species, to safeguard his country and help propagate the natural species which are within his sacred domain.

The anthropologist Theodor Strehlow lived for much of his life in Central Australia, and was closely associated with the Aranda (Arrernte) people who accorded him initiatory privileges. As a result, he was able to gain valuable insights into the ceremonial life of the Aranda men in particular. Strehlow presents as an example of the transformative process an Aranda man who is a member of the Krantji clan — all of whom believe they are incarnations of a Kangaroo Spirit Ancestor. This man has passed through circumcision rites which have earned him membership of the clan in the first instance, and he has also been given the secret name of the Kangaroo Spirit Ancestor which now dwells within his very being as a living presence. In addition he has been given a *tjurunga* object as a token of his totemic status and has been shown a dramatic performance which is uniquely associated with his personal Kangaroo Ancestor. He now knows the sacred verses which accompany this performance and these have been assigned to him as his 'property'. Until his death only he is allowed to perform this act and sing these verses, unless he authorises his personal assistants to do so.[25]

Strehlow describes an Aranda (Arrernte) ceremony where initiated members of the Krantji clan sing the songs associated with the Kangaroo Ancestor and then allow sacred blood from their arms to pour down upon the Earth, as a sign that the life force from the Spirit Ancestor is fertilising the Earth. The kangaroo men then sing further Krantji songs as they construct a large 'ground picture' in the earth:

After the completion of the ground painting, a ceremonial phallus or para was constructed by all men who were members of the kangaroo totemic clan and it was fastened in turn upon the head of every kangaroo performer who approached the clan ground painting in order to blow into its central hole. This procedure was repeated over a number of weeks until all the kangaroo totemic ancestors who featured in the clan ceremonial cycle had been revealed to the assembled members of the totemic clan. Finally the phallus was brought into contact with the ground-painting by the whole group of kangaroo men, and the down from it was stripped into the central hole of the ground painting. Meanwhile it was covered with down stripped from the ground painting, and finally branches were heaped upon the down-filled hole. The men would leave the ceremony confident that through the re-enacting of the original Krantji creative rite by the human reincarnations of the Krantji kangaroo totemic ancestors to the singing of the Krantji sacred verses, the ground painting would once again give birth to hundreds of kangaroos after the next heavy summer rains had fallen.[26]

It is apparent from this ritual that new 'kangaroo life' can only come forth from the Earth when some of the life force from the original Kangaroo Spirit Ancestor is poured upon it. However, in a ceremonial sense, the blood which flows from the arm of a man who belongs to the Krantji kangaroo totem is equivalent to the life force of the actual Ancestor, and achieves the same result.

An important consideration here, too, is that the Krantji kangaroo men are doing more than simply increasing the number of kangaroos upon the Earth. By celebrating their totem through their ceremonial performance they are also increasing the potency of the Spirit Ancestor's life essence at their ceremonial site, and in so doing they enhance the Ancestor's life essence within themselves.

A RITUAL FOR RESOLVING CONFLICT

As we have seen, Aboriginal groups by their very nature are often scattered across large sections of the country, but their rich ceremonial life helps to bond them together — especially when they share custodianship of different parts of a major myth cycle.

Before ceremonies are performed, it is not uncommon for men who have major grievances with their neighbours, to air them publicly. Sometimes this may lead to a fight, but later the conflict will be resolved and apologies accepted. In some parts of the country there are specific rituals for resolving conflict. The example given below is for the most part 'men's work', but once again the women in the community also play a part in the proceedings.

The Nathagura Fire ceremony of the Warramunga people in northern Central Australia is essentially about releasing tension. It is a way of acknowledging the cumulative stress associated with quarrels and disputes, working through them, and then resolving them — a type of 'purification by fire'. An account of this fire ceremony is provided by Baldwin Spencer and F. J. Gillen, who were among the first white explorers to document Aboriginal ritual life. Spencer was Professor of Biology at the University of Melbourne and went as a member of the Horn scientific expedition to Central Australia in 1894. In Alice Springs he met F. J. Gillen, who was the post and telegraph master there. Together they collaborated

on a number of studies on Aboriginal life and culture, including the book *The Northern Tribes of Central Australia*, first published in 1904, which contains details of the Warramunga Fire ceremony. The following is an abbreviated version which nevertheless contains the main details:

The Nathagura Fire ceremony is run by members of the *Kingilli* moiety, but before it begins there are long sessions of unruly behaviour where the men dance around the campfire adopting grotesque poses, hurling insults at each other, calling each other by incorrect skin names and addressing the women by their personal names — something they would never do normally. Similarly, young boys steal food from the older men and run away with it — an act of quite atypical, disrespectful behaviour.

In the morning there is a type of reconciliatory dance, with the women initially dancing by themselves but then, through their gestures, inviting the men to participate as well, in an undulating line formation. Later in the evening there are further dance revelries, more insults, and more wild grotesque posturing. However, no one is supposed to take offence at any of this, for it is a deliberate, ritually sanctioned inversion of the way things normally are among the Warramunga people. The basic intention of the fire ceremony is to bring all these types of conflicts out into the open and then resolve them, so they are no longer a part of day-to-day concerns.

A few days after the opening revelries a number of Kingilli men then set to work to make twelve large *wanmanmirri* torches, each consisting of a long pole surmounted by dry gumtree twigs that are easy to ignite. These torches play a central role in the fire ritual itself.

Just prior to the commencement of the ceremony the twelve men who have been assigned to carry the *wanmanmirri* torches — men with deep grievances to vent — daub themselves all over with red mud and then smear a further coating of white pipe clay on top of the mud, giving themselves a very ghoulish appearance. When each man is ready, the torches are set alight.

The performance begins with one man charging with his flaming torch towards another man against whom he holds a serious long-standing grievance. The second man in turn is surrounded by other men brandishing clubs and spear throwers, and they help deflect the burning torch upwards as it is thrust towards them. The torch confrontations continue and soon 'the whitened bodies of the combatants were alight with burning twigs and leaves. The smoke, the blazing torches, the showers of sparks falling in all directions and the mass of dancing, yelling men with their bodies grotesquely bedaubed, formed altogether a genuinely wild and savage scene...'

After this intense confrontation, however, the *wanmanmirri* torches were dashed upon the ground and extinguished, bringing hostilities to an end. A period of silence followed, and the men then washed the mud and embers from their bodies, and sat around the campfire singing peacefully together.

While the Fire ceremony had been proceeding, the women in the community had slept on the ground some distance away. Just before sunrise, the men stopped their singing, came towards the place where the women were resting, and threw small pieces of lighted bark in their direction to announce that the ritual had now ended.

When Baldwin and Spencer asked the elders to explain what had just taken place there was a very straightforward and uncomplicated response: 'All that the old men could tell us was that it had been handed down to them from the far past just as it used to be performed by their Alcheringa ancestors.' The object of the Fire ceremony was to finally settle old quarrels and to make everyone well disposed towards one another.[27]

As we have seen, in Aboriginal culture both women and men share the sacred trust that is the living legacy of their Spirit Ancestors. Their Law acknowledges that women's and men's roles complement each other, and both are respected — whether we are considering such roles as gathering food, looking after children, or performing rituals and passing on their sacred knowledge to present and future generations. Aboriginal women and men alike recognise that both have an important contribution to make to their society. For what is most significant to all Aboriginal peoples is the survival of their ancient culture and the wisdom of the Eternal Dreamtime.

I got to be buried at the South Alligator [River]

In that big banyan tree...

Then after one or two years, take my bones and paint them.

Paint them with red ochre first.

Then take them back to Cannon Hill, Back to Warriyangal... In the cave.

Leave my bones at Warriyangal.

Leave them for good...

Forever.

Then I can see my dreaming from the cave.

That good.[1]

Chapter Eight

LIFE CYCLES

For Aboriginal peoples, birth, life and death are part of an eternal cycle of renewal which is continually replenished by the vitality of the Spirit. In the broadest sense of the term, the life cycle begins with Spirit and returns to Spirit, but in a purely physical sense — when one is considering the life of a particular human being — it extends from conception and birth through to death.

The cycle of physical life for each individual person extends through different phases which entail entering a pre-existing social structure and passing through various stages or transitions which are sometimes known as 'rites of passage'. In the case of a young girl, she will make a transition through puberty to the stage of becoming an adult woman, and then in all likelihood will marry and bear children. She will also increasingly engage in the rich ceremonial life of 'women's business', and perhaps in due course will become a senior Law woman within the group. A young boy, meanwhile, will pass through his first rites of initiation at puberty — rites which usually involve circumcision — and will gradually become involved in the spiritual heritage shared by initiated male members of the group. He may then aspire to become a senior Law man.

All of these phases, however, are social transformations within an eternal spiritual process, for all human beings owe their life to the animating force of the Spirit Ancestors. Without them nothing could live, and the World would be devoid of meaning.

CONCEPTION, BIRTH AND YOUTH

For Aboriginal people conception is a fusion of physical and spiritual events. There are two aspects to the Aboriginal idea of conception. Sexual intercourse between a woman and a man will result in the creation of a new mortal 'life' and this is seen as part of the natural order of physical reproduction. However, what is more important is the role of the child's spirit. When the woman has actually become pregnant, a Spirit Ancestor may then incarnate in the foetus as a spirit child, and it is this spirit child which is directly linked to the Dreamtime. This incarnation of the Spirit Ancestor thus provides the animating 'spirit' for the foetus — without which it would die. It is this spirit which is immortal.

Opposite: Aboriginal man and child with song sticks at Daly River, Northern Territory. Courtesy of Wildlight.

Opposite: Pitjantjatjara children at
Ernabella in central Northern
Territory. Courtesy of Wildlight.

Across the country there are different 'spirit centres' — usually waterholes — where the spirit children dwell. These spirit children have different terms according to the language of the tribal group. Some people say that these spirit children may be visible around the campfire but disappear when you get too close. A woman who wishes to give birth to a spirit child may go to one or other of the spirit places and perhaps swim in the waterhole or river and sit there with her legs apart so that one of the spirit children may enter her. Perhaps one of them might also follow her back home to the camp.

'Conception' takes place when the spirit child enters the womb, and the 'conception place' is identified as the place where the woman first feels her baby move inside her. Alternatively it may be a place where the father has a dream that his wife is pregnant and announces this to be so. Either way, the conception place is extremely important in Aboriginal cultures because it brings with it rights to land, and establishes the child's sense of place within the group. Paternity is established by a man's relationship to the mother of the child.

Although children are among the most cherished possessions of both women and men, there is little ritual or ceremony around the actual childbirth. In traditional Aboriginal life, childbirth must take place away from the main camp, perhaps in a windbreak shelter, and is considered strictly married women's business. Usually the mother-to-be is attended to by particular other women such as her co-wives (explained at page 174), her husband's mother or her own mother's mother if she is living in close enough proximity. Generally speaking, although childbirth is an important event in terms of the continuation of the species, the process itself — provided there are no complications — is a no-fuss affair. One reason why there is little ritual around the birth of a child is that the event cannot be accurately timed to occur at a certain time of the year. Initiation ceremonies, for example, are often held during the seasons which bring abundance, in order to cater for guests. With childbirth it is different — the timing is not always anticipated.

In contemporary times, Aboriginal women have tried to avoid giving birth to their children in modern western hospitals because this may complicate a child's birthright and its specific links to totemic territory. However, if there is no option but to give birth in a hospital, Aboriginal women will nevertheless endeavour to include some traditional ritual practices immediately after the birth. Diane Bell mentions that at Warribri, '. . .as soon as the mother leaves hospital, the [Aboriginal] women take her and the child away into the bush where they perform certain rituals to ensure the health and growth of the child and the renewed strength of the mother.'[2]

A widespread ritual in Aboriginal women's health practices is 'smoking the baby' soon after childbirth, which marks the beginning of a child's ceremonial life. Smoking is an important cleansing and purifying rite and forms part of, and the conclusion of, many rituals — for birth, at times of sickness and death and also to purify the habitats and belongings of the deceased. After childbirth a mother will smoke both herself and her baby as part of the ritual cleansing which also includes burial of the afterbirth. In this ritual, specific preparations, wood and plants are involved in the making of the purifying fire. In the Kimberleys, for example, the leaves of the konkerberry bush are used because they emit a healing vapour. After smoking herself, the mother reverently holds the baby over the smoking leaves of the fire for a brief period — often face downwards so that it will be of a well behaved disposition. The umbilical cord, which is

Pitjantjatjara child.
Courtesy of Wildlight.

GIVING BIRTH: A DREAMING STORY

This women's myth from the Wik Munggan people describes the birthing procedure as laid down in the Dreamtime by the black snake man and his wife the dove:

Yuwam the black snake and Kolet the dove were once husband and wife and lived by a river, travelling up and down its banks. The wife is heavy with child and when her time comes upon her, she sits down while her husband goes away. She kneels, sitting on her knees as the contractions begin. The head appears and she guides the baby out and onto the ground. She holds the cord and begins calling out names. She calls names one after the other until the cord gives way and then she knows that she has found the baby's proper name. She repeats this name as the afterbirth comes out. All is over and she lays the baby on a sheet of paperbark.

The man comes back and sits a short distance from her. 'I wonder what it is,' he says, as if to himself. 'It's a man child,' she says, as if to herself. She sits by herself, then lies down. The baby cries and she gives him her breast.

For five days the mother lies resting. Her husband brings her yams, always the same, but neither of them eat any fish, lest the baby grow sick and die. The husband cooks the yams and lays them a little way off from his wife. After five days, she says aloud to herself, 'It is finished.' The man goes fishing, catches some fish. He lights the fire, breaks the neck of the fish and cooks them. He eats a small catfish and a knight-fish, then lays some aside for the evening meal. The woman now goes to look for her own yams. As the fluid is still flowing, she is not allowed to eat fish. She is not allowed to eat any of the fish her husband catches, nor can he eat any of the yams she digs up.

After about six days, when the woman's flow stops, she can take the baby to her husband. She puts the yams and some small fish she has caught into three dilly bags, filling them right to the top. One bag is for herself, one is for her husband and the third is for the baby. She has made a string apron and puts this on. She smears her face with clay and her body with ashes, putting white clay on her forehead. She rubs charcoal over the baby's body and a white smear of paint on his nose. She breaks off the navel cord to give to her husband. She fastens a beeswax pendant to it, striped with strips of yellow bark, and then ties the cord around the neck of the baby. Picking up the dilly bags, she hangs one from her head, slings another across her shoulder and her chest to hang under the arm, then places the third one on her head. She then goes to the father.

She lies the baby in his arms and after a time he smears it with sweat, rubbing it over the forehead and face. He then takes the cord and places it around his own neck. The mother places the yams beside her husband, then picks up a dilly bag and rubs it across the mouth of the baby, so that he will not always be crying. Finally, she lies on her stomach, saying, 'So that he will not always be running after others for food, but will come running back to us, and we will always keep together.'

After this, in this Dreamtime story, the woman, the dove, Kolet, returned to her own *djang* or *auwa* place and the black snake man and his son returned to his.[3]

said to possess magical properties, is put in a special dilly bag which the mother wears around her neck for a while, after which it passes via a close relative to the father who includes it in a sacred dilly bag. In many regions, to ensure a baby is darkly coloured like other family members, it is rubbed with ashes.

NAMING THE CHILD

In addition to all the mythic and totemic considerations referred to earlier, the importance of the child's link with the land can also be seen through the bestowing of names. Individual names are usually given by senior family members, like a grandparent, and are carefully chosen so that they indicate which descent and land-owning group the child belongs to. It may be that the name refers to a particular Spirit Ancestor, or a particular location on the family's land, or it may refer to some feature of the land, sea or sky — for all of these may feature as part of individual Dreamings. The name that is given is used until puberty, when the child is initiated and receives a new name — and then the first name will be remembered as a 'secret name' and not referred to generally at all. For day-to-day purposes, Aboriginal people prefer to use the general kinship names like 'sister' or 'brother', or sometimes even 'whitefella' names, because these are not serious names and have no totemic or symbolic ramifications within their culture.

Children belong to the whole community once they are born — for as we have seen they have many classificatory mothers and fathers. However, in day-to-day terms a child will generally spend most of its time with its mother, or with someone who takes on her role.

Babies generally sleep in a curved wooden dish or are wrapped in paperbark. Even as the child grows older it will still sleep around the campfire with its mother and this pattern will generally continue till puberty. Each child knows who its actual father is, but from another perspective it has several fathers, because the father's brothers are also known by the name 'father' — and they in turn all share the responsibility of helping the child to develop and acquire useful skills. In this way a child gradually participates more and more in the life of the community and quickly becomes part of a daily routine.

The child will have to either stay with its grandparents or go with its mother while she digs for yams or forages for bush tucker — but all the time the child is observing and learning from what is going on all around. Children soon learn which foods are gathered and which plants avoided, how to make a fire, what the various bush tracks indicate, and how to catch accessible creatures like lizards or shellfish, depending on the natural resources of the locale. A young child will also learn from the older children, and will pick up fragments of the spiritual traditions as well — through songs, and by listening around the campfire to general talk about the Ancestors, ghosts and spirits. Children also learn about sexuality by being open about it. From time to time they may indulge in erotic fun among themselves, and imitate in games that they have seen adults do quite freely. There is a certain indulgence of young children in all respects, and punishments, when applicable, are more often threatened by their parents than carried out.

It is interesting that in some traditional groups even though young boys are obviously very dependent on their mothers, even by the age of five or six they may be encouraged to separate out a little from their mothers, and perhaps become a bit more independent — even to the extent where the young boys may begin to express hostility towards their mothers and also

Paperbark tree.

towards their sisters. While this behaviour may be condoned by the men in the extended family, it is generally not allowed to go too far. In general, a young boy will remain very much part of his mother's domain until he leaves for the bachelor's camp around the age of twelve or thirteen, and a girl will similarly remain very much within her mother's group until the stage of puberty and marriage.

BECOMING A WOMAN

In Aboriginal society a girl takes the first step in being acknowledged as a woman when she menstruates for the first time. Menstruation itself was introduced by the Ancestors — such as the Djan'kawu Sisters themselves who have deemed menstrual blood as *maraiin*, or sacred. Thus menstruation is no ordinary occurrence but rather has mythical sanction. It also has a certain inherent magical potency for in this instance blood has flowed forth naturally from the body onto the ground — something which men imitate in a number of rituals. Menstrual blood is a source of *djang*, and among the Wik Munggan people it is associated with the Rainbow Snake and with the magic shaman serpent, Taipan. Mudrooroo describes a Dreamtime story from this group of people which explains the link between Taipan and women's fertility, blood and milk:

> Yuwam, the black snake with red under its belly, ran away with Ita the swamp-fish man, who was in the category of 'son' to her husband, Tintauwa, the black water snake, and thus they were committing incest. Taipan, as her mother's brother and upholder of the Law, followed to punish this 'wrong way' relationship. He caught up with her and created a bog or swamp around her so that she could not escape, although Ita managed to run away.
>
> Yuwam had daughters who were swimming in a lagoon nearby. They were completely hairless and had no breasts or organs, or periods. Taipan went to them and the whole area turned red. The frightened girls tried to hide, rubbing mud over their heads, their chests and between their legs. They dove under the water and later emerged to find that they had long hair on their heads, tufts under their arms and pubic hair. They also had breasts.
>
> Yuwam, the mother, tried to rise from beneath the bog she had been trapped in, but could not. She kept sinking deeper and deeper. Taipan said to her, 'My girl, my sister's daughter, you have received this punishment from your mother's earth.' He smoothed a spot and pulled out some grass and said, 'Some blood, I have brought you woman. The rest I will carry windward and spill there at my sacred place.' He made a hole in the ground for the blood he gave to the woman and put it there for her. This became 'forbidden' ground. It was at the foot of a bloodwood tree — the menstrual blood. Taipan said that Yuwam would become a snake with a red belly and so she did.
>
> He also put some milk at the foot of a milkwood tree and said, 'When women are grown up, milk shall come to them all from this milkwood tree. People everywhere will come to this place, to this tree for babies. You will give a girl baby to the women who come here. Girl babies will come from this fertility place of yours, Yuwam.' And Yuwam sank beneath the surface and the place is sacred to her and is a fertility site for women who want girl babies.[4]

In traditional Aboriginal communities there are small-scale ritual procedures following a girl's first menstruation. She must then leave the main camp where she has been living with her mother, and now goes to live in a small hut or shelter some distance away. Here she will spend time in seclusion, perhaps observing certain food taboos. From time to time some of the older women will come to visit her, and they will tell her various myths related to her transition to womanhood, and might also give her advice on what to anticipate when she gets married.

After her period of seclusion the girl returns to the main camp, decorated in red ochre, and may go down to a nearby billabong or river at daybreak to bathe ritually with a crowd of girls. Following her ritual bathing and her reception back at the camp it is now assumed that she has become a woman.

Amongst the Kukatja peoples in desert regions of Western Australia, the women ritually honour the Tjipari song cycle which is a rite of passage account of the travels of two Ancestral Women — two Nangala Sisters — who begin their journey as girls and are later transformed into women. As they journey south to north-east they give name to the country and all that they see. They tell of the country they pass through, and their deeds, as they hunt, make camp, paint their bodies, sing and dance. Through body painting, songs, dances and sacred boards of Tjipari, the travels of the two Sisters, the Nangalas, are celebrated by Aboriginal women. The ceremonial songs and dances of Tjipari celebrate both the physical and spiritual journey of the women — honouring the land, the travelling and the 'business' of transformation whereby the Nangala sisters journey from girlhood to womenhood. Mirlkitjungu Millie Skeen of the Wirrimanu community (Balgo Hills) relates the story of her Tjipari Dreaming painting, reproduced on the following page.

> In the Ngarangkarni (Dreaming), two Nangala (skin name) Sisters left their mother to travel across the country, learning the land and growing up as women. The two sisters travelled far, having many adventures along the way. They stopped at soakwaters where they dug for water and found food. In carrying out the ceremonies sacred to those places, they painted themselves in pilytji (red) and karntawarra (yellow) ochre and adorned themselves with the white headdresses used today by women in Tjipari ceremonies. As they travelled, they changed the country about them. They hid from a storm in one place, and in another, they ran away from a bushfire. Those places are marked by land formations today. By the end of the journey they had become women.[5]

Once a girl has made her right of passage to womanhood, and is she has already been betrothed, her marriage arrangements will now be made. She now has a different status within the group. She has become a mature young woman, is no longer dependent on her mother, and is potentially able to have children of her own.

There are some major social implications for the young woman's mother as well, for she may soon become a mother-in-law — a significant role in Aboriginal society. And the transition marked by puberty is also important for the young woman's grandmother. If a betrothal has already been arranged some fifteen years earlier, confirming the forthcoming arrangements will be partly her responsibility. It is likely, too, that the grandmother will be called upon to attend the young woman when she first gives birth to a child.

Although young women often married after puberty, it should be mentioned that this did

not necessarily mean that every young woman would immediately cohabit and engage in a sexual relationship with her husband. In traditional Aboriginal society, certain sexual restraints have been generally observed by both men and women as a natural method of restricting the population, thus ensuring that the number of mouths to feed was commensurate with available resources.

It was not unusual, for example, for a young women to live for a time at the single women's camp until it was considered by her relatives that she was old enough to move in with her husband, and even if she spent time in this camp, this would not necessarily mean that the marriage had been sexually consummated. Both women and men exercised control over their sexuality. Also, forms of natural birth control were adopted in traditional communities as a matter of course. Aboriginal women preferred to space the births of their children, so the period spent breastfeeding an infant was often quite extensive, thus repressing ovulation. Married couples often practised voluntary celibacy from time to time as well — periods which would vary according to need and region. The fact that women and men sleep in different camps, following the gender demarcations which are observed in traditional camp life, also has an effect on the number of children that are born. In the past it has been generally agreed that the size of families should be contained, and a comparatively high rate of infant mortality was condoned as a way of maintaining an appropriate population balance according to resources and the related need for seasonal mobility. With the forced move from traditionally mobile camp life to settlements such practices have become more difficult to observe.

The act of giving birth, although a powerful individual experience, has a significance that is much greater in its connection to the universal and greater design of the Dreamtime and all that this entails. Women in their roles as mothers, nurturers and custodians of Dreamtime Law practise their ritual traditions and 'grow up' country and kin throughout the course of their daily lives. Their custodial roles increase as their children become older and more independent, when their time is largely spent as respected elders involved in all aspects of major decision making in their communities. Senior Law women, as repositories of cultural knowledge, are very powerful — both in their communities and in their ritual life known as women's business. Elderly women are also often able to witness the rituals of men that were taboo when they were younger — for a certain relaxation of the normal rules may then apply. Women continue to spend considerable time teaching children the Dreamtime Law that infuses every aspect of life, and thus act as key wisdom keepers and transmitters of their culture.

BECOMING A MAN

Being male in Aboriginal society brings with it very specific rites of passage and particular kinship and social obligations, and these begin from birth. As we have seen, each child has a totemic relationship with the land, and its totem is identified by and associated with the Spirit Ancestor into whose 'country' the child was born. It cannot be assumed, though, that if the child is male, it will automatically grow up and acquire rights to the father's spiritual and custodial bond with the land. Aboriginal people do not believe, for example, that a 'boy grows up' — as white Australians might express it. Instead they say that the boy was 'made a man' in his first initiations conducted by the senior Aboriginal men. The act of growing up doesn't happen by itself in Aboriginal society. Obviously a male child will develop physically, and in the

Opposite: *Tjipari Dreaming* by Mirlkitjungu Millie Skeen, a Kukatja Law woman, of the Wirrimanu (Balgo Hills) community. Mirlkitjungu relates the Tjipari story of this painting: 'In the *Ngarangkarni* (Dreaming), two Nangala (skin name) sisters left their mother to travel across the country, learning the land and growing up as women. The two sisters travelled far...stopped at soakwaters, where they dug for water, and found food. In carrying out the ceremonies sacred to those places, they painted themselves with *pilytji* (red) and *karntawarra* (yellow) ochre and adorned themselves with the white headdresses used today by women in Tjipari ceremonies. As they travelled, they changed the country about them...Those places are marked by land formations today. By the end of the journey they had become women.' Courtesy of Manungka Manungka Women's Association.

normal course of growth will become taller and stronger and acquire more practical skills with the passage of time. But these natural processes are not, of themselves, sufficient. In Aboriginal culture one does not pass from boyhood to manhood until society itself proclaims that this transition has taken place. There is a specific path, or rite of passage, from youth to manhood — and it is marked by initiation. Only through initiation does a boy become a man.

This major transition occurs around twelve or thirteen years of age. Until this time the older men in the group will have watched the boy's development with interest, and when they feel he is ready for the first stages of initiation he is then taken away — with the parents' consent — to live instead with other boys of a similar age and status in a 'bachelors' camp'. According to the anthropologist W. E. H. Stanner, who lived with the Murinbata people in the Port Keats region of the Northern Territory, boys taken away to bachelor camp were no longer referred to by their personal names but were now called 'wild dogs' until their first initiation was over.[6]

Across Aboriginal Australia there are broadly similar practices in the male initiation process, although specific details may vary from place to place. In the first instance, the young boy is invariably taken away from the camp of his parents to another place of seclusion and isolation. In some Aboriginal groups the women make a show of crying and may also brandish spears in an act of mock defiance for the 'loss' of the child at this time. But it would appear that this is a symbolic response rather than a statement of personal anguish — for the women know full well that their sons must pass through to the next phase of life. Once the boy is taken away he may be daubed in part with red ochre or with human blood, and in some instances a shell might be hung around the boy's neck to mark his role as a 'novice'. Then, in due course the boy may be presented to other groups of men who will be involved in the boy's subsequent initiation ceremonies.

At the time of the first initiation, various groups will come to the appointed place, fix their camps, and enter into the general welcome of the *corroboree* — a public celebration associated with exuberant dancing, wild animal cries, enthusiastic clapping, rhythmic beating of percussion instruments, and much stamping of feet. The *corroboree* sets the tone of something dramatic about to happen and also provides a meeting place where points of discussion, betrothal negotiations and even major grievances between different groups, can be aired openly and resolved prior to engaging in the major ceremony.

Across the country various body-practices have served as prelude to initiation. It was not uncommon in New South Wales, for example, for an upper incisor tooth to be knocked out prior to initiation — a practice which appears on the basis of archaeological evidence to have continued for at least 8000 years. In Western Australia, meanwhile, Aboriginal groups would tie the arms of novices with painful ligatures and keep them on for several days, as a test of character and strength. In northern Queensland several groups would mark a man's arms and back with cicatrices, or ritual cut-marks. It has been something of a tradition among senior Aboriginal men that the 'secrets' should not be passed across too easily — that young boys need to experience pain and learn endurance in their path to manhood.

Across Aboriginal Australia most initiations are also characterised by a period of seclusion, and it may be that this period represents a symbolic withdrawal from the everyday world and the now tangible beginnings of the venture into sacred territory. Sometimes youths from the bachelor camp spend these periods of seclusion together — each helping the other to find food — although they are sometimes allowed to receive food which has been sent specially from their parents' camp. At this time they are not allowed to return to the camp themselves, but are often allocated an instructor or guide who can guide them through their ordeal of separation, and provide support where necessary. The boys are told not to reveal anything they have learned or seen during this period of seclusion.

It is also a characteristic feature of Aboriginal initiations that in addition to procedures like circumcision there should also be a blood ceremony. This generally involves cutting a vein in the arm and allowing blood to flow from the body, down upon the earth. Aboriginal peoples consider arm blood to be sacred and it is used ceremonially both for daubing the body and also for sacramental drinking — both by the newly initiated candidates and also the officiating elders. At this time special songs are also sung to accompany the drawing of blood. Aboriginal people believe that arm blood, through its vital essence, fortifies the initiation candidates and prepares them for the ordeals associated with receiving sacred knowledge — an ongoing process of learning which lasts for many years. Red ochre is sacred to Aboriginal people for the same reason: it is like blood from the Spirit Ancestors which can cure, protect and provide strength.

GETTING MARRIED

In traditional Aboriginal society getting married is not just a matter of the heart. Obviously in modern society many Aboriginal people have chosen to marry non-Aboriginal partners and have taken on a number of 'whitefella ways' in making their marriage choices. However, in a traditional context it was different because kinship considerations played such a major part in the selection process. Here, even allowing for various bargaining procedures involving senior women and men in the community, individuals were restricted in their choice of marriage partners, and the welfare of the social group was generally considered more important than individual choice.

Various issues were involved in selecting a marriage partner. As we have mentioned earlier, one could not marry a member of the same clan totem or moiety group, and if there were further subsections within the group one would not be allowed to marry within those groups either. As a consequence a man would often marry a woman whom we would call a 'cross cousin' and who was also a member of the correct skin group. This would often be his mother's father's daughter or his father's sister's daughter, allowing for accepted rules within the group, and making allowance for the broad classificatory system of kin terms that has already been described.[7]

In addition to these considerations, however, it is important to remember that in traditional Aboriginal groups women have been rightly regarded and accepted as full members of their societies. They are also highly valued for a number of reasons, not the least of which is their 'revered and feared' capacity to bear children, and their ability to provide the major part of the family's food — both of which are acknowledged as vital for human survival. Given these imperatives, it was not uncommon in past times for children to be betrothed in infancy or even before they were born. Girls were also sometimes promised from infancy to older male partners as a way of forging alliances between different groups. A sense of

Opposite: *Sick, Dying, Mourning*
by Paddy Fordham Wainburrnga, a
Rembarrnga man from central
Arnhem Land. Courtesy of Co-ee
Aboriginal Art.

reciprocity would often enter into these negotiations, so that a group granting their approval for a woman to marry might expect to receive a bride in return at some future time.

Generally speaking, betrothal marriage arrangements have always been seen as part of a complex web of kinship obligations and social responsibilities. And while a young woman would not find an older man a very exciting marriage prospect, a marriage of this sort was unlikely to be a lifetime contract. Also if a woman's first husband was considerably older, it might well be that 'sweetheart' relationships would be officially allowed. If the male partner were to die before a marriage was consummated it was not uncommon for the young woman to then marry the man's brother closest in age — although a woman's right to have a say in matters of marriage such as this was respected. Also, because of humiliations that could and did occur in the cases of big age differences in marriage, an older man might choose to live in the single men's camp.

In some areas of the country, too, it is permissible for a man to have several wives, although it would appear in these cases that the reasons have less to do with sexual prowess than with issues of economics, prestige and political alliances. In these cases, co-wives (or co-sisters) have generally enjoyed positive relations — supporting each other and sharing responsibilities. Women too are known to sometimes have relationships with younger men for the rejuvenating effect it brings, but this does not always extend to marriage. And although women were not permitted to have more than one husband at a time, they could have several husbands in the course of a lifetime. As long as a woman remained fertile, a number of people would be interested in her 'marriageability' for a number of reasons.

There are few accounts of homosexuality in traditional Aboriginal life, possibly because there was the expectation, among all regional groups, that every boy and girl would marry in due course. Such an expectation, of course, carried a heterosexual emphasis within the society. There is also little information on how many 'first' marriages endured until the death of one or other of the spouses, though these commitments did (and still do) occur — as did the dissolution of marriage though the latter were not formalised as 'divorce' in a western sense. Polygamous marriages — where a man could have more than one wife — were accepted in traditional Aboriginal life, though it was less commonly practised than monogamy. Aboriginal marital and family units differed in practices according to regional groups and affiliations. However, these units were more flexibly defined and certainly existed in less isolation than their western counterparts. It was generally understood and accepted that increased expectations, responsibilities and obligations were part of marriage and family life. Reciprocity prevailed in family life, as it did in other social relations.

Women have traditionally expected to have a husband and this principle is respected and accommodated within the community. Men have obligations in this matter and even if marriage partners are not attracted to each other, a woman would be granted her expectation that her husband supply her with meat, and be included as his wife in all kinship obligations and social matters. Only if a woman was very old could this right be waived, and she could then choose to live permanently in the single women's camp. Other possibilities and renegotiations have also been widely practised.

Traditionally, women were also known to exercise a major influence in marriage outcomes by other means — such as negotiations at times of initiations and at other gatherings. In addition, they were able to use the power of their rituals and ceremonies — such as the *yilpinji* of the Central Australian women. The use and potency of the *yilpinji* love songs to direct attention towards prospective male partners was often seen to be effective. However, this practice was only exercised in terms of relationships that were socially sanctioned and within the 'right skin' kinship terms and allegiances.

As mentioned earlier, the event of marriage itself was not generally accompanied by substantial rituals, although there would usually be an exchange of gifts between the new husband and the family of the bride to cement the new relationship. However, it was basically the fact of a couple living together publicly that would constitute the 'marriage'. Sometimes a woman's husband would initially come to live with the bride's parents for a few years, to assist them with food gathering and in other supportive capacities, and then the couple would move to the husband's traditional land or 'country'. At other times, if a woman's mother's mother was available to assist her in childbirth, it appears that a woman would remain in her birthplace, or live nearby. In any case, a married couple would generally, though not universally, set up camp and live and sleep together until the first child was born. At this stage, as we have already seen, the gender-based demarcation would then begin to take place within the campsite, with an area around the fire put aside for the mother and children on the one hand, and another area allocated to the father.

In traditional life, women's and men's roles were treated with respect and there were a number of checks and balances within the society so that neither gender could have unrivalled dominance over the other. Similarly there were reprisals, or the threat of them, from family members, to deter maltreatment of one person by another. Traditionally, Aboriginal women and men also enjoyed roles that entertained a considerable degree of flexibility so there were variations in practices, even within groups as well as in different regions. All of these factors and practices

Senior Law woman,
Yuelamu community,
Mount Allen, Northern
Territory.

have been dramatically affected and altered by the intrusions of western cultural dominance and the enforced movement into the 'frontier colonial societies' that constitute settlement life.

GROWING OLD

A traditional Aboriginal person who attains the age of fifty-five to sixty years may well be classed as an 'elder' within the family group. Though age is not the sole criterion of the status of 'authoritative elder', rather it is a demonstrated knowledge of ritual business and decisive leadership skills through the course of adult life which is more recognised. For example, as Catherine Ellis points out, a knowledgable person in terms of traditional culture is defined as the person 'knowing many songs', for without song knowledge, information about places, laws, correct behaviour, healing, food sources and a host of other items is unavailable[8]. Middle-aged people also could wield considerable authority either by becoming a camp leader or through a particular initiation to become a tribal 'doctor' or traditional healer — a *mullamullin* among the Kurnai Koori people, for example — or a 'clever' man or woman. Traditional healers (often called shamans or medicine men and women) were known by different names according to the language of a group but *maban, kadaicha, ngangkayi, mekigar, wirrnum* and *birraark* are some of the names ascribed to them. Psychic ability — such as telepathy and clairvoyance — is quite common in Aboriginal cultures, but traditional doctors have powers above these 'norms' and thus they hold considerable status as people of 'high degree' within their societies. There were and are male and female 'doctors' or healers, and in both cases it is not a simple matter of choosing one's path — particular abilities have to be present and skills acquired. Jandamarra, the great warrior of the Punuba people — also known as Pigeon — and White Lady, a Koori woman who lived in the nineteenth century, are two examples of famous traditional healers.

The physical act of getting old, however, brings with it both joys and disappointments. An older man, for example, might find it increasingly difficult to hunt the larger animals and may come to depend almost completely on the efforts of his sons and his daughters' husbands. But this is considered to be a fair trade within the reciprocal rules of Aboriginal culture. Adult daughters and sons are expected to bestow the same support and care upon their ageing parents as they themselves received as dependent children. Elderly women, meanwhile, seem to forage and collect bush tucker for many more years than the men hunt, and are often very supportive of each other.

There seem to be widespread instances, at any large campsite, of a few elderly men living together in a cluster and small groups of senior women similarly living by themselves in the single women's camp — security and companionship in this instance being provided by 'strength in numbers'. With the transition from family group camps to frontier settlement life, complications have arisen in all matters to do with human relationships. The single women's camp, which now houses separated and divorced women, visiting women, and the older powerful women, continues to wield considerable influence in any settlement.

Generally speaking though, age — sadly unlike western cultures today — does bring with it seniority and respect. Both older women and men alike can command considerable influence within their respective groups. For elders, the ability to command respect hinges primarily on the secret ritual knowledge which they possess and authoritively execute. They subsequently

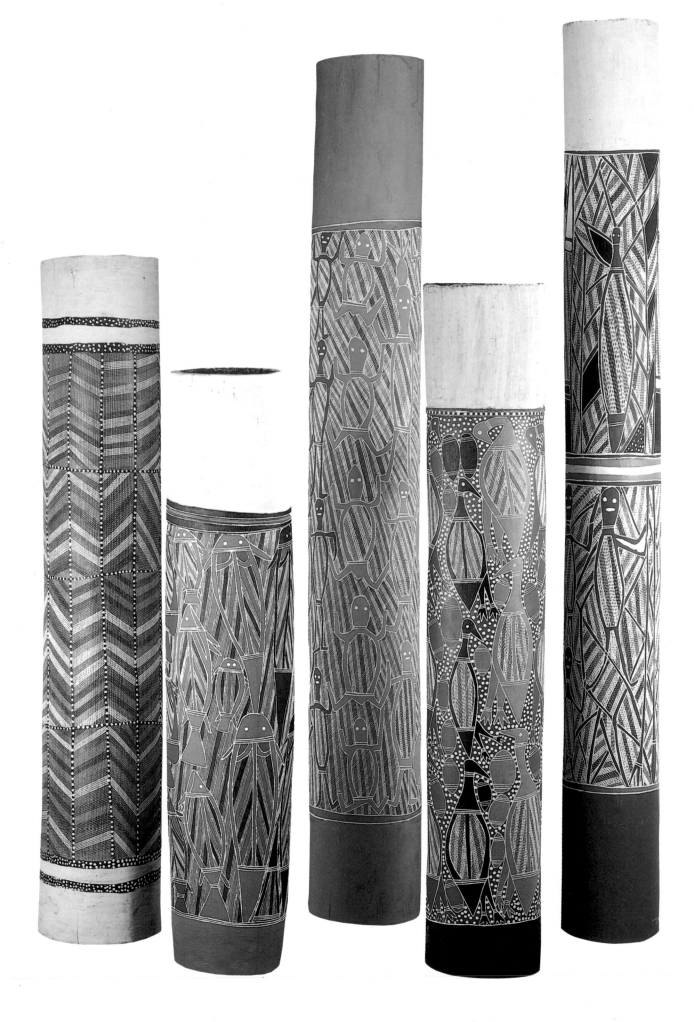

have both the position and the responsibility to pass this knowledge on to future generations — and this in turn has a direct bearing on the initiatory rites of passage that affect all the younger people within the group. With this passing on of knowledge rests the continuation of Aboriginal cultural traditions and its millennia of accumulated wisdom. Knowledge of the song cycles and ritual business, rather than material goods, are the most valued and desired possessions for Aboriginal men and women and it is this prime criterion that distinguishes women and men of 'high degree' in Australian Aboriginal cultures.

Elders, in this sense, are indeed the most esteemed members of the culture for they are the repositories of applied cultural knowledge and the wisdom keepers of the Dreamtime legacy — in them rests the trust, hope and continuance of present and future generations of Aboriginal traditions. The fractures of white colonisation have of course threatened the very existence of the legacy of these ancient living traditions and with it the knowledge necessary for the continued survival of this land and her species. Nevertheless, it is with this awareness that Aboriginal peoples, displaying their typically resilient and adaptive natures, are now using western media tools to record and thus preserve the testimonies of those elders who know first-hand the traditional ways in order to preserve their most treasured inheritance.

DEATH AND THE SPIRIT WORLD

The end of the life cycle of course brings death, but for Aboriginal peoples this inevitability means a transition rather than an ending — all of which is transcribed in the events of the Dreamtime. Although having personal and ritual meaning, death, like all dimensions of Aboriginal existence, is an accepted part of the ongoing and eternal cycle of creation and destruction — of conception, birth, growth, maturity, decline, death and rebirth — provided that the correct rituals are faithfully and continuously observed. As a person dies, so do other species with which they are connected: the seasonal cycles of vegetation, the Sun and the Moon and so on. Moon in particular is important in beliefs about death, as Moon was the first Ancestral Spirit to die. Also featuring prominently in death — with the exception of very young infants, the very old or the activity of environmental elements — is sorcery. Deaths in the cases of youth or middle-age are considered unnatural — hence someone is believed to be responsible and recompense has to be exacted. After the disposal of the body and its accompanying rituals — called 'sorry business' in English — an inquest is sometimes held to determine responsibility and punishment in the case of an 'unnatural' death, though this is dependent to some extent on the standing of the deceased and the ability or readiness of close kin to take potentially provocative revenge.

Death, like birth and all transitions or life crises in Aboriginal Australia, is marked by ritual and ceremonial practices, such as the Morning Star ceremony or the *lorrokon* of the Gunwinggu (or *Kunwinjku*) of Arnhem Land. Initiations throughout the course of life are regarded as 'deaths' in the sense that they mark the end of one period of being and the birth of a new stage in the life cycle. So there are several deaths and rebirths in Aboriginal and Torres Strait Islander cultures which prepare people for the final passing — or the initiation of return — from the physical plane to the realm of spirit. Soon after the death of the physical body, the spirit departs the material plane and re-enters the spiritual realm — either going to the Land of the Dead — such as Bralgu (or Bralku) in Arnhem Land (from whence

Opposite: Hollow log coffins (or lorrokon) from Maningrida in Arnhem Land. Courtesy Coo-ee Aboriginal Art.

the Djan'kawu Beings originated) — or returning to the Earth and spirit places such as waterholes before awaiting rebirth once again into physical form. Rebirth depended on circumstances in the physical world, and when a Spirit Ancestor sought to reincarnate they could assume either the form of a human being or some other creature, for all are held equal in the Aboriginal belief system.

The tensions of this final phase are seen to reside in the desire of the spirit wanting to both stay in close proximity to loved ones and to return to the Spirit World. The same could be said of certain relatives or close kin of the deceased, so the period immediately following a physical death is seen as potentially threatening, and for this reason precautions are deemed necessary. The social implications of death can be extensive and despite the raw everyday knowledge of death as part of life, and the acceptance of the ongoing life of the spirit, there is loss and distress in the deaths of particular individuals. In addition to personal grief, there is the heightened awareness of one's own physical mortality and the possible presence of sorcery — so it is a time of keenly felt vulnerability in a camp. Also, in the traditional pattern of living, after a death had occurred everyone had to abandon camp and the deceased person's belongings were either destroyed or ritually cleansed. In this way, everyone within a community was affected in one way or another.

The specifics of death and mortuary ritual vary according to tribal affiliation. However, there are some similarities of behaviour throughout Aboriginal Australia, a few of which can be mentioned. Generally there is much wailing and crying among close relatives — actual and symbolic — with some relatives gashing themselves and drawing blood. The hair of the corpse may also be plucked to make sacred *rangga*. Because of its spiritual connections, ritual blood can also be used in other aspects of a burial ritual — as can its symbolic equivalent, red ochre. It is also common for close relatives of the deceased to cut their hair. People within the camp, or who live in other camps, and who may have some connection with the deceased are notified as quickly as possible for a body, when it is available, has to be quickly disposed of — particularly in the warmer regions of the country. Mourning rites, or 'sorry business' can also be undertaken at camps other than where the body awaits ritual disposal.

A corpse is disposed of in various ways such as burial, mummification, cremation, or exposure in a tree or high platform — or it may be placed in a hollow log. In some parts of Australia the sacred chants of a person's totemic clan group are sung to assist the spirit on its return to its spirit home. Similarly, totemic designs are painted on the log coffin or container holding the exhumed or retrieved bones of the deceased so a spirit knows where to return. A log coffin or container is then left by itself in the landscape to decay naturally, as is the way of physical life. The ritually prepared bones could also be taken to the source of the deceased person's spirit — the sacred waterhole. Bones of the deceased have to be carefully monitored and prepared to guard against possible malevolent use in sorcery. These latter events mark the final phase of mortuary ritual, and the entire procedure can last from a few months to a few years.

A widespread observance amongst Aboriginal peoples is that a deceased person's name is not mentioned and no subsequent reference is made to them, except in special circumstances. For example among the Warlpiri, the word *kumunjayi* (no name) is a substitute term for a deceased person and the necessary observances. Memory of that person will of course continue, and it may well be that the deceased person begins to feature at a later stage in sacred songs — or in other ceremonial contexts. Spirits of the dead are known to visit and communicate information to relatives in dreams. This information can be of a personal nature relating to the death, or some other matter, and the spirit may also impart songs and ritual information. A well-known example of this is the *Krill Krill* (or *Gurirr Gurirr*) ceremony which was given to eminent Australian artist Rover Thomas in a series of visionary dream visitations by a recently deceased female relative — killed in a car accident as a result of the storm conditions created by Cyclone Tracy. Dreams of this nature appear to be more likely to happen soon after a person's passing.

Although traditionally the deceased — and any reminder of them, including their name — is ritually removed from any physical contact with those physically living, they are certainly not forgotten. If death is traumatic, it is also transitory. Aboriginal people do not consider physical death to be final because the body is simply a 'temporary manifestation'. Although a death marks the end of a particular set of relationships in this life, the spirit, on the other hand, is linked forever to the Dreamtime and the Spirit Ancestors — and is eternal.

ENDNOTES

Introduction

1   James Barripang, of the Golpa tribe, lives on Marchinbar Island and is primary custodian of the Golpa territory and traditions; quoted in Stephen Davis, *Above Capricorn*, Angus and Robertson/Harper Collins Publishers (NSW), 1994, pp. 99, 101.

2   Scientists have recently proved that the 'Bradshaw style' paintings are at least 17,000 years old. This has been achieved through analysing sand grains enclosed in petrified wasps' nests built over the Bradshaw paintings.

3   *Bringing Them Home*, 'Report of the National Enquiry into the Separation of Aboriginal & Torres Strait Islander Children from their Families' by the Human Rights and Equal Opportunity Commission, Commonwealth of Australia, 1997.

4   See Max Charlesworth, Richard Kimber and Noel Wallace, *Ancestor Spirits*, Deakin University Press, Geelong (VIC), 1990, p. 81.

5   See Anna Voigt, *New Visions New Perspectives*, Craftsman House, Sydney, 1996, p. 218.

6   Mumballa Mountain is south of Bermagui in New South Wales.

7   Permission was given by Guboo Ted Thomas to Anna Voigt to quote his 'Renewing of the Dreaming'.

8   Quoted in W. E. H. Stanner, *White Man Got No Dreaming*, ANU Press, Canberra, 1979.

9   Quoted in: 'Desert Tracks - Pitjantjatjara Tours' by Diana James in Susan Hawthorne and Renate Klein (eds), *Australia For Women*, Spinifex Press, North Melbourne, 1994, p. 330.

Chapter One: Creation

1   David Mowaljarlai and Jutta Malnic, *Yorro Yorro*, Magabala Books, Broome (WA), 1993, p. 132.

2   For an explanation of the word 'myth' see pages 36-8.

3   See T. G. H. Strehlow, 'Australia', in C. J. Bleeker and G. Widengren (eds), *Historia religionum*, vol. 2, Brill, Leiden, 1971, pp. 613-14.

4   Eddie Kneebone, 'An Aboriginal Response' in Catherine Hammond (ed), *Creation Spirituality and the Dreamtime*, Millennium Books, Newtown (NSW), 1991, p. 89.

5   Mudrooroo, *Aboriginal Mythology*, Aquarian Press, London, 1994, p.52.

6   Oodgeroo Noonuccal and Kabul Oodgeroo Noonuccal, *The Rainbow Serpent*, AGPS Press, Canberra, 1988.

Chapter Two: Myths of the Eternal Dreamtime

1   Oodgeroo Noonuccal, 'The Beginning of Life', in *Stradbroke Dreamtime*, rev. ed., Angus and Robertson, Sydney, 1993, pp. 59-60.

2   Ibid., pp. 59-61.

3   Christine Adrian Dyer (ed), *Kunwinjku Art from Injalak 1991-1992*, Museum Art International, Adelaide, 1994, p. 58.

4   See Ronald M. Berndt, *Djanggawul*, Routledge and Kegan Paul, London, 1952, p. xvii.

5   Baldwin Spencer, *Native Tribes of the Northern Territory of Australia*, Macmillan, London, 1914, pp. 276-8.

6   Anna Voigt, *New Visions New Perspectives*, op. cit., p. 192.

7   Ibid., p. 203.

8   Oodgeroo Noonuccal, *Stradbroke Dreamtime*, op. cit., pp. 64-5.

9   T. G. H. Strehlow, *Aranda Traditions*, University of Melbourne Press, Melbourne, 1947, pp. 7-10.

10 Christine Adrian Dyer, *Kunwinjku Art*, op. cit., p. 50.

11 Ibid., p. 94.

12 See Charles Mountford, *The First Sunrise*, Rigby, Adelaide, 1971, p. 30.

13 Catherine H. Berndt, *Land of the Rainbow Snake*, Collins, Sydney, 1979, p. 18.

14 Ibid., pp. 14-15.

15 Quoted in Judith Ryan, *Images of Power*, National Gallery of Victoria, Melbourne, p. 11.

16 Mudrooroo, *Aboriginal Mythology*, Aquarian Press, London, 1994, pp. 175-6.

17 Judith Ryan, op cit., p. 11.

Chapter Three: Sacred Earth Sacred Land

1   Anne Pattel-Gray, *Through Aboriginal Eyes*, World Council of Churches Publication, Geneva, 1991, pp. 2-3. Anne Pattel-Gray was the first Aboriginal person to obtain a PhD in Religious Studies. She is founder and executive secretary of the Aboriginal and Islander Commission of the National Council of Churches in Australia.

2   Yami Lester, *Yami*, Institute for Aboriginal Development Publications (IAD), Alice Springs (NT), 1993, p. 10.

3   Galarrwuy Yunupingu, 'Concepts of Land and Spirituality', presented at the first National Conference on Aboriginal Spirituality and Perceptions of Christianity, *Aboriginal Spirituality: Past, Present and Future*, South Australia, 1990.

4   Quoted in *The Aboriginal Gift*, Eugene Stockton, Millennium Books, Alexandria (NSW), 1995, p. 82.

5   Ronald M. Berndt and Catherine H. Berndt, *The Speaking Land*, Inner Traditions International, Vermont, USA, 1994, p. 5.

6   W. E. H. Stanner, 'Religion, Totemism and Symbolism', in R. M. and C. H. Berndt (eds), *Aboriginal Man in Australia*, Angus and Robertson, Sydney, 1965, p. 215.

7   David Mowaljarlai and Jutta Malnic, op. cit., p. 137.

8   Eugene Stockton, op. cit., p. 56.

9   David Mowaljarlai and Jutta Malnic, op. cit., pp. 190-2.

10 Bill Neidjie, *Story About Feeling*, Magabala Books Broome (WA), 1989, p. 3.

11 Reproduced in *My Mother the Land*, edited by the Galiwin'ku Literary Production Centre, Elcho Island, quoted by Eugene Stockton in *The Aboriginal Gift*, op. cit., p. 82.

12 M. R. Ungunmerr-Baumann, 'Autobiographical Reflections', *Nelen Yubu*, no.28, 1986, pp. 13-18.

13 A. Pattel-Gray, *Through Aboriginal Eyes*, op. cit., p. 2.

14 Ibid., pp. 2-3.

15 Quoted in J. Roberts, *Massacres to Mining*, Dove Communications, Melbourne, 1981, p. 148.

16 Quoted in Chelsea Hotel Magazine, vol. 7. no 1, Eggingen, Germany, 1995.

17 Ibid.

18 Alex Grey, *Aboriginal Family Education Centres: A Final Report to the Bernard van Leer Foundation 1969-1973*, Department of Adult Education, University of Sydney, 1975, p. 28.

19 Mudrooroo, *Aboriginal Mythology*, op. cit., p. 131.

20 Quoted in sleeve notes, *Ochres* CD soundtrack, composed by David Page, 1995.

21 Mudrooroo, op. cit., p. 138.

22 Ibid., p. 102.

23 Gondwanaland is the name of the ancient land-mass believed to have existed in the southern hemisphere which included Africa, India, Australia and South America.

24 Bill Neidjie, op. cit., pp. 80-1.

25 Mudrooroo, op. cit., pp. 169-170.

26 Ibid., pp. 90-1.

27 Mowaljarlai and Malnic, op. cit., p. 138.

28 A. P. Elkin, *The Australian Aborigines*, Angus and Robertson, Sydney, 1948, p. 138.

29 Anna Voigt, *New Visions New Perspectives*, op. cit., pp. 192-9.

Chapter Four: Song Line, Music and Dance

1   Anna Voigt, *Forty Thousand Divided By Two Hundred Unequals . . .*, 1988, p. 2.

2   Quoted in *Before the White Man*, Readers Digest, Sydney, 1974, p. 19.

3   Richard M. Moyle, *Songs of the Pintupi*, Aboriginal Studies Press, Canberra, 1979.

4   Catherine J. Ellis, *Aboriginal Music*, rev. ed., University of Queensland Press, St. Lucia, 1993, p. 48.

5   Ibid., p. 70.

6   Ibid., pp. 70-1.

7   Catherine J. Ellis and Judith Martyn-Ellis, 'The Sung World of Aboriginal and Islander Women' in Susan Hawthorne and Renate Klein (eds), *Australia for Women*, op. cit., p. 165.

8   Catherine J. Ellis, *Aboriginal Music,* op. cit., p. 154.
9   R. M. Berndt, *Djanggawul,* op. cit., p. xxi.
10 Catherine J. Ellis, *Aboriginal Music,* op. cit., p. 73.
11 Anna Voigt, *New Visions New Perspectives,* op. cit., pp. 192-6.

Chapter Five: Ritual and Ceremony

1   Bill Harney — Wardaman Tribesman from the Katherine region, Northern Territory;
    quoted in James Cowan and Colin Beard, *Sacred Places in Australia,* Simon and
    Schuster Australia, East Roseville (NSW), 1991, p. 102.
2   Jean A. Ellis, *Australia's Aboriginal Heritage,* Collins Dove, Melbourne, 1994 p. 30.
3   Richard Moyle, *Alyawarra Music,* Australian Institute of Aboriginal Studies,
    Canberra, 1986, p. 151.
4   Diane Bell, *Daughters of the Dreaming,* McPhee Gribble/Allen and Unwin,
    Sydney, 1983, p. 21.
5   Ibid., pp. 125-8 .
6   Ibid., pp. 125-8.
7   Ronald M. Berndt, *Djanggawul,* op. cit., p. xvii.
8   See Ronald M.Berndt, *Djanggawul,* op. cit.
9   Ronald M. Berndt and Catherine H. Berndt, *Man, Land and Myth in North
    Australia,* Ure Smith, Sydney, 1970, p. 114.
10 Ibid., pp. 117, 120-1.
11 Ibid., pp. 135-142.
12 Sorcery or the threat of sorcery is ever present in Aboriginal life — particularly
    in matters to do with health, sickness, death and revenge — and there are many
    practices which surround these beliefs.
13 Ronald M.Berndt and Catherine H. Berndt, *The World of the First Australians,*
    Aboriginal Studies Press, Canberra, 1992, pp. 286-7.
14 Les Hiatt, *It's About Friendship — Rom: a Ceremony from Arnhem Land,*
    Aboriginal Studies Press, Canberra, 1994, p. 5.

Chapter Six: Totem, Kin, Family and Survival

1   David Mowaljarlai in *Yorro Yorro,* op. cit., p. 137.
2   See Ronald M. Berndt and Catherine H. Berndt, *The World of the First
    Australians,* op. cit., pp. 232-3, 237.
3   John von Sturmer in 'Talking with Aborigines', *AIAS Newsletter,* No. 15,
    Canberra, 1981, p. 13.
4   Petronella Vaaron-Morel (ed), *Warlpiri Women's Voices,* IAD Press, Alice Springs
    (NT), 1995, p. xiv.
5   Isobel M. White, 'Sexual Conquest and Submission in the Myths of Central
    Australia' in L. R. Hiatt (ed), *Australian Aboriginal Mythology,* Australian
    Institute of Aboriginal Studies, Canberra, 1975, p. 136.
6   See Diane Bell, *Daughters of the Dreaming,* op. cit., p. 284.
7   Peter Latz, *Bushfires and Bushtucker,* IAD Press, Alice Springs (NT), 1995, p. 22.
8   Penny Van Oosterzee, *The Centre: The Natural History of Australia's Desert
    Regions,* Heinemann, Melbourne, 1991, p. 100.
9   Quoted in Jordan Crugnale (ed), *Footprints Across Our Land,* Magabala Books,
    Broome (WA), 1995, p. 143.
10 Ibid., p. 143.
11 Ibid., p. 2.
12 Ibid., p. 22.
13 Ibid., p. 68.
14 Peter Latz, op. cit., p. 22.

Chapter Seven: Women's Business, Men's Business

1   Kathleen Petyarre, quoted in Anna Voigt, *New Visions New Perpectives,* op, cit.,
    p 221.
2   Phyllis M. Kaberry, *Aboriginal Woman: Sacred and Profane,*
    Routledge, London, 1939.
3   Catherine Berndt from the 1950s into the 1990s; Jane Goodale in 1971; Isobel
    White in 1970 and 1975; and Diane Bell from 1983 into the 1990s. See
    Bibliography.
4   T. G. H Strehlow, *Aranda Traditions,* Melbourne University Press,

    Melbourne, 1947, p. 94.
5   See Ronald M. Berndt and Catherine H. Berndt, *The World of the First Australians,*
    op. cit., p. 256-7.
6   Catherine J. Ellis and Judith Martyn-Ellis, 'The Sung World Of Aboriginal and
    Islander Women' in Susan Hawthorne and Renate Klein (eds), *Australia For
    Women* op. cit., p. 164-5.
7   Quoted in 'Women's Business is Hard Work', in Max Charlesworth et al (eds),
    Religion in Aboriginal Australia, University of Queensland Press, St. Lucia, 1984,
    p. 345.
8   This categorisation of 'owners' and 'managers' is common throughout Aboriginal
    Australia.
9   Quoted in Anna Voigt, *New Visions New Perspectives,* op. cit., p. 221.
10 Ibid., p. 224.
11 Ibid., pp. 223-4.
12 Diane Bell, 'In the Tracks of the Munga-Munga', submission to Cox River Land
    Claim, Darwin, Northern Land Council, 1982b.
13 Ibid.
14 See Diane Bell, *Daughters of the Dreaming,* op. cit.
15 Diane Bell, op. cit., p. 164.
16 Ibid., p. 168.
17 Ibid., p. 130.
18 Ibid., pp. 168-9.
19 T.G.H. Strehlow, *Songs of Central Australia,* Angus and Robertson,
    Sydney, 1971, p. 476-7.
20 Nancy Munn, *Warlbiri Iconography,* Cornell University Press, Ithaca and London,
    1973, p. 47.
21 Diane Bell, Max Charlesworth et al (eds), op. cit., p. 355.
22 Ian Keen, *Knowledge and Secrecy in an Aboriginal Religion,* Clarendon
    Press, Oxford, 1994, pp. 174-5.
23 A. P. Elkin, *The Australian Aborigines,* Angus and Robertson, Sydney, 1948, p. 161.
24 Ibid., p. 163.
25 T. G. H. Strehlow, *Central Australian Religion,* Adelaide, 1978, p. 26.
26 Ibid., p. 28.
27 Baldwin Spencer and F. J.Gillen, *The Northern Tribes of Central Australia,*
    Macmillan, London, 1904, p. 392.

Chapter Eight: Life Cycles

1   Felix Holmes —last senior man of the Limilngan Tribe and custodian of the
    Mordak mortuary song cycle, which connects the sites and territory of several
    other tribes in the Kakadu area with tribes around Darwin — quoted in Stephen
    Davis, *Above Capricorn,* op. cit., pp. 35, 41.
2   Diane Bell, *Daughters of the Dreaming,* op. cit., p. 151.
3   Mudrooroo, *Aboriginal Mythology,* op. cit., p. 28.
4   Ibid., p. 105.
5   Anna Voigt, *New Visions New Perspectives,* op. cit., p. 202.
6   W. E. H. Stanner, *White Man Got No Dreaming,* ANU Press, Canberra, 1979, p. 348.
7   See C. Bourke et al, *Aboriginal Australia,* University of Queensland Press,
    St. Lucia, 1994, p. 89.
8   Catherine J. Ellis and Linda Barwick, 'Antikirinja Women's Song Knowledge
    1963-72' in Peggy Brock (ed), *Women Rites & Sites,* Allen and Unwin,
    St. Leonards (NSW), 1989, p. 21.

SELECTED BIBLIOGRAPHY

Bell, Diane, *Daughters of the Dreaming,* McPhee Gribble/Allen and Unwin, Sydney, 1983.

— 'Women's Business is Hard Work' in Max Charlesworth et al (eds), *Religion in Aboriginal Australia,* University of Queensland Press, St Lucia, 1984.

— 'In the Tracks of the Munga-Munga', submission to Cox River Land Claim, Darwin, Northern Land Council, 1982b.

Berndt, C.H., *Land of the Rainbow Snake,* Collins, Sydney, 1979.

Berndt, R.M., *Djanggawul:An Aboriginal Religious Cult of North-Eastern Arnhem Land,* Routledge and Kegan Paul, London, 1952.

Berndt, R.M. and Berndt, C.H. (eds), *Aboriginal Man in Australia: Essays in Honour of Emeritus Professor A. P. Elkin,* Angus and Robertson, Sydney, 1965.

— *Man, Land and Myth in North Australia:The Gunwinggu People,* Ure Smith, Sydney, 1970.

— *The Speaking Land,* Inner Traditions International, Vermont, USA, 1994.

— *The World of the First Australians:Aboriginal Traditional Life, Past and Present,* Aboriginal Studies Press, Canberra, 1992.

Bourke,C., Bourke, E. and Edwards, B. (eds), *Aboriginal Australia,* University of Queensland Press, St Lucia, 1994.

Brock, Peggy (ed), *Women Rites and Sites:Aboriginal Women's Cultural Knowledge,* Allen and Unwin, St Leonards (NSW), 1989.

Charlesworth, M., Kimber, R., Wallace, N., *Ancestor Spirits:Aspects of Australian Aboriginal Life and Spirituality,* Deakin University Press, Geelong (VIC), 1990.

Charlesworth, M., Morphy, H., Bell, D., Maddock, K., (eds), *Religion in Aboriginal Australia,* University of Queensland Press, St Lucia, 1984.

Crugnale, Jordan (ed), *Footprints Across Our Land,* Magabala Books, Broome (WA), 1995.

Cowan, J. and Beard, C., *Sacred Places in Australia,* Simon and Schuster Australia, East Roseville (NSW), 1991.

Davis, Stephen, *Above Capricorn:Aboriginal Biographies from Northern Australia,* Angus and Robertson/Harper Collins Publishers, Pymble (NSW), 1994.

Dixon, R.M.W. and Koch, Grace, *Dyirbal Song Poetry:The Oral Literature of an Australian Rainforest People,* University of Queensland Press, St. Lucia, 1996.

Dyer, Christine A.(ed), *Kunwinjku Art fom Injalak 1991-1992,* Museum Art International, Adelaide, 1994.

Eliade, M., *Australian Religions:An Introduction,* Cornell University Press, Ithaca and London, 1973.

Elkin, A.P., *Aboriginal Men of High Degree,* 2nd Edition, University of Queensland Press, St Lucia, 1977.

Elkin, A.P., *The Australian Aborigines,* Angus and Robertson, Sydney, 1948.

Ellis, Catherine J., *Aboriginal Music,* rev. ed., University of Queensland Press, Brisbane, 1993.

Ellis, Catherine J. and Martyn-Ellis, Judith, 'The Sung World of Aboriginal and Islander Women' in Susan Hawthorne and Renate Klein (eds), *Australia for Women,* Spinifex Press, North Melbourne, 1994.

Gale, F. (ed), *We are Bosses Ourselves:The Status and Role of Aboriginal Women Today,* Australian Institute of Aboriginal Studies, Canberra, 1983.

Grey, A., *Aboriginal Family Education Centres:A Final Report to the Bernard van Leer Foundation 1969-1973,* Department of Adult Education, University of Sydney, 1975.

Hammond, Catherine (ed), *Creation Spirituality and the Dreamtime,* Millennium Books, Newtown (NSW), 1991.

Hiatt, L.R. (ed), *Australian Aboriginal Mythology,* Australian Institute of Aboriginal Studies, Canberra, 1975.

Human Rights and Equal Opportunity Commission, *Bringing Them Home: Report of the National Inquiry into the Separation of Aboriginal and Torres Strait Islander Children from Their Families,* Commonwealth of Australia, 1997.

Kaberry, Phyllis M., *Aboriginal Woman: Sacred and Profane,* Routledge, London, 1939.

Keen, Ian, *Knowledge and Secrecy in an Aboriginal Religion,* Clarendon Press, Oxford, 1994.

Latz, Peter, *Bushfires and Bushtucker,* IAD Press, Alice Springs (NT), 1995.

Lester, Yami, *Yami:The Autobiography of Yami Lester,* Institute for Aboriginal Development Publications, (IAD), Alice Springs (NT), 1993.

Mowaljarlai, David and Malnic, Jutta, *Yorro Yorro: Spirit of the Kimberley,* Magabala Books, Broome (WA), 1993.

Moyle, Richard M., *Alyawarra Music: Songs and Society in a Central Australian Community,* Australian Institute of Aboriginal Studies, Canberra, 1986.

Moyle, Richard M., *Songs of the Pintupi: Musical Life in a Central Australian Society,* Aboriginal Studies Press, Canberra, 1979.

Mudrooroo, *Aboriginal Mythology,* Aquarian Press, London, 1994.

— *Us Mob,* Angus and Robertson, Sydney, 1995.

Munn, Nancy, *Warlbiri Iconography: Graphic Representations and Cultural Symbolism in a Central Australian Society,* Cornell University Press, Ithaca and London, 1973.

Neidjie, Bill, *Story About Feeling,* Magabala Books, Broome (WA), 1989.

Oodgeroo Noonuccal, *Stradbroke Dreamtime,* rev. ed., Angus and Robertson, Sydney, 1993.

Oodgeroo Noonuccal and Kabul Oodgeroo Noonuccal, *The Rainbow Serpent,* AGPS Press, Canberra, 1988.

Pattel-Gray, A., *Through Aboriginal Eyes: The Cry From The Wilderness,* World Council of Churches Publications, Geneva, 1991.

Roberts, J., *Massacres to Mining: the Colonisation of Aboriginal Australia,* Dove Communications, Melbourne, 1981.

Rutherford, Anna (ed), *Aboriginal Culture Today,* Dangaroo Press - *Kunapipi,* Sydney, 1988.

Ryan, Judith, *Images of Power,* National Gallery of Victoria, Melbourne.

Spencer, Baldwin, *Native Tribes of the Northern Territory of Australia,* Macmillan, London, 1914.

Spencer, Baldwin and Gillen, F. J., *The Northern Tribes of Central Australia,* Macmillan, London, 1904.

Stanner, W. E. H., 'Religion, Totemism and Symbolism' in R. M. Berndt and C. H. Berndt (eds), *Aboriginal Man in Australia: Essays in honour of Emeritus Professor A. P. Elkin,* Angus and Robertson, Sydney 1965.

— *White Man Got No Dreaming,* ANU Press, Canberra, 1979.

Stockton, Eugene, *The Aboriginal Gift: Spirituality for a Nation,* Millennium Books, Alexandria (NSW), 1995.

Strehlow, T. G. H., *Aranda Traditions,* University of Melbourne Press, Melbourne, 1947.

— 'Australia' in C. J. Bleeker and G. Widengren (eds), *Historia religionum,* vol.2, Brill, Leiden, 1971.

— *Central Australian Religion,* Adelaide, 1978.

— *Songs of Central Australia,* Angus and Robertson, Sydney, 1971.

Ungunmerr-Baumann, M. R., 'Autobiographical Reflections', *Nelen Yubu,* no.28, 1986.

Vaaron-More, Petronella (ed), *Warlpiri Women's Voices,* IAD Press, Alice Springs (NT), 1995.

Voigt, Anna, *New Visions New Perspectives: Voices of Contemporary Australian Women Artists,* Craftsman House, Sydney, 1996.

von Sturmer, John, *Talking with Aborigines,* AIAS Newsletter No. 15, Canberra, 1981.

White, Isobel M., 'Sexual Conquest and Submission in the Myths of Central Australia' in L R Hiatt (ed), *Australian Aboriginal Mythology,* Australian Institute of Aboriginal Studies, Canberra, 1975.

PHOTOGRAPHIC CREDITS

Photographer	*Page No.*
Beard, *Colin*	43, 52, 152-3
Castleton, *Philip*	48, 93, 170
Cummings, *Steve*	33, 47, 84, 116, 182-3
Dalton, *Tina*	132
Drury, *Nevill*	71, 28-9
Johns, *Carolyn*	Back Cover, 100-1, 135
Lourie, *David*	37, 51, 96
McLeod, *Neil*	Front Cover, 83
McGlone, *Julie*	34, 80
Moore, *David*	163, 164
Quirk, *Philip*	85, 119
Rankin, *Andrew*	112-3
Turner, *Grenville*	62-3, 89, 90, 98-9, 102, 136, 139, 157, 160, 176
Voigt, *Anna*	Endpapers, Introduction, 8, 20-1, 25, 26-7, 28-9, 30, 40, 58, 59, 64, 65, 67, 68, 72, 74-5, 129, 140, 144, 145, 167
Walker, *Robert*	86, 109

INDEX